on the diet track.
today
yes
today

[GHOST NOTES]

Other Books by Michael Corcoran

All Over the Map: True Heroes of Texas Music

The Sanctified Soul of Arizona Dranes

Washington Phillips and His Manzarene Dreams

[GHOST NOTES]

PIONEERING SPIRITS OF TEXAS MUSIC

Michael Corcoran

Illustrations by Tim Kerr

TCU Press

Fort Worth, Texas

Library of Congress Control Number:2019957058

Published with support from the
Center for Texas Music History
at Texas State University
and Record Town.

Design by Bill Brammer

Photos of Tim Kerr's art by Sandy Carson

TCU Box 298300
Fort Worth, Texas 76129
817.257.7822
www.prs.tcu.edu
To order books: 1.800.826.8911

Ghost notes are barely audible
and unseen,
a wisp lingering around the beat,
yet somehow driving the
groove

CONTENTS

PART 4: Rock 'n' Rap

PART 5: Moguls and Mentors

Preface

Mack McCormick never finished the book everyone wanted him to write. The music historian, who passed away in November 2015 at age eighty-five, knew more about Robert Johnson than anyone else. He knew more about Fourth Ward piano players and East Texas songsters and the blues divas who sang in whorehouses. He knew where the story started and how it ended, in detail that would take years to collect, and yet the middle part, the writing, drove him nuts. Research was one of his two main passions; writing was the other. In his thoughts he was a historian, but when he sat down at the typewriter he became more than that. Or maybe less.

Diagnosed with bipolar personality, the Houston-based McCormick accomplished much amidst his inner mental distress. He found Mance Lipscomb and Robert Shaw, recording them for the first time as old men. He managed the unmanageable Lightnin' Hopkins and mentored Chris Strachwitz of the Arhoolie label (named by Mack) in gritty native Texas music. But most of all, McCormick dug deep to find connections, painstakingly tracing back to the source.

At his memorial service in Houston, McCormick was eulogized by some of those who've taken up his work. Andrew Brown, who's written extensive liner notes for Bear Family boxed sets, described a high school dropout who became an intellectual, an eternal outsider who got close to the flame. He was "the man who cared too much."

Another protégé, Roger Wood (*Down in Houston*), recalled how McCormick loved to solve the puzzle of poetry. His favorites were Emily Dickinson and Walt Whitman, and Wood quoted each. Dickinson's "The truth must dazzle gradually or every man be blind" spoke of McCormick's steady thoroughness.

"I am large," Wood read from a Whitman poem McCormick once quoted to him. "I contain multitudes."

The time I went to Mack's house in Houston, he almost turned me away after I mentioned another music historian who, it turned out, Mack had a beef with. (Not unusual.) This was in 2003, and I was researching Blind Willie Johnson. Eventually Mack calmed down and we had passable Mexican food and strong margaritas at a nearby restaurant. "I think Blind Willie Johnson is, one day, going to be like Robert Johnson, known more for who he influenced than what he did on his own," said McCormick, who considered Blind Willie as much a blues musician as gospel. "What makes Pentecostal singers different from, say, Baptist singers?" he asked, apologizing for his lack of study in the religious music field.

I drove back to Austin the next day seeing that big hole as an opportunity to make my own mark as a gospel music historian. If McCormick had already researched an area it would be like hitting a garage sale at noon.

Forget the flashy and famous, was McCormick's advice to me. Find the originators and tell their stories.

Most of these chapters started as newspaper or magazine articles, where footnotes are not used. Some of this research goes back twenty years and was included in my liner notes for reissues by Arizona Dranes and Washington Phillips and the 2016 tribute LP *God Don't Never Change: The Songs of Blind Willie Johnson*, featuring Tom Waits and others. I've tried my best to retrace the research and cite sources, and apologize for any instance of failing to credit. But there's so much misinformation out there on these humble virtuosos that I rarely went with just one source for each fact. Consensus and common sense were vital to this endeavor which, although imperfect, is as accurate as I could make it.

Getting the correct information amid conflicting accounts is an obsession with me, but as I wrote in the intro of this book's prequel *All Over the Map*, this is history, not science.

BLUeS
truth
Washington Phillips
Blind Willie Johnson
Arizona Dranes

PART 1

Gospel

CHAPTER 1

Goin' to See the King

The Holy Trinity of Texas Gospel Pioneers

The rocker, the singer-songwriter, the guitar hero all sprang from these fully formed musicians, who recorded before any of the more celebrated Mississippi Delta deities. And yet, because they played gospel, not the more collectable and researchable blues, Arizona Dranes, Washington Phillips, and Blind Willie Johnson had been woefully bypassed by musicologists and historians until recently.

They were from 1920's Black Church, Texas, and created soulful sacred music that linked Negro spirituals and Gospel's Golden Age. Listen to their versions of "Bye and Bye, I'm Goin' To See the King," the only song all three recorded, and you'll hear that Arizona Dranes, Washington Phillips, and Blind Willie Johnson each had their own sound. But in unison, they brought a new intensity and introspection to records, influencing not only church, but popular music too. They were there when the "sorrow songs" of the Antebellum South were set free by the beat of the blues and the elation of gospel.

Dranes put secular piano styles to wild, congregational rhythm, which set the template for rock 'n' roll. Phillips was a farmer who built an ethereal sound on scraps and morals and had one of his songs covered by Linda Ronstadt in her prime. Blind Willie Johnson wrote the rules of bottleneck guitar and bellowing bass vocals. But the liner notes for '90s reissues of Dranes, Phillips, and Johnson read like elaborate riddles—and most of the clues were wrong.

History Never Gets Old

Over the past decade and a half, I came to spend months at a time with each of their histories, but I discovered all three on the same day. Dranes, Phillips, and Johnson were knockouts on a British knock-off compilation called *Amazing Gospel*, which I received in a clump of packages at the *Austin American-Statesman* in 2001. Leadoff track "My Soul Is a Witness" by Dranes, Phillips's parobolic "A Mother's Last Words To Her Daughter" (his version of "Bye and Bye"), and Blind Willie's "Nobody's Fault But Mine," which I had thought was a Led Zeppelin original, are the cuts that stayed with me from the first listen. When I found, via essential gospel histories *How Sweet the Sound* by Horace Boyer and Anthony Heilbut's *The Gospel Sound*, that they were all from Texas, the state where I've been a music journalist for over thirty years, I started searching deeper.

In the beginning of a pop music critic career, you're chasing the next big thing, with the fantasy you'd be like Jon Landau, discovering "the future of rock 'n' roll" in some club. But as you get older, you realize that you can also discover someone who's been dead sixty years. Someone whose music influenced those who influenced Bruce Springsteen.

This is the story of the children of former slaves, who found the God-given grace within themselves to make music that was as much about liberation as it was about faith. They were of the earth and formed from the injustice of the time. And yet there's a spiritual purity in their music that comes from a place we dream about.

A Race to Make Records

Thomas A. Edison invented the phonograph in 1877, but the production of "entertainment records" didn't start until 1888. The first popular African American recording artists in 1901 were Bert Williams and George Walker, a former minstrel act billed as "The Two Real Coons" because they didn't need to wear blackface (though they did for heightened comedic effect). Their records on the Victor Talking Machine label appealed to whites.

It wasn't until Mamie Smith sold half a million copies of "Crazy Blues" in 1920 to a black audience that had migrated to the cities for jobs during WWI that record companies were convinced African Americans would buy records in quantity. They bought them, in fact, at a higher rate than whites, which nascent record men Ralph Peer (who supervised the "Crazy Blues" session for OKeh), Frank B. Walker of Columbia, and Art Satherley of Paramount were quick to capitalize on.

With Walker discovery Bessie Smith coming along in 1923, plus Ethel Waters, Ma Rainey, Sippie Wallace, Victoria Spivey, Ida Cox, and more on the "race records" charts, blues recordings were predominantly sung by females at first. A 1924 poster for Papa Charlie Jackson's "Salty Dog Blues" boasted "this man can sing and play the blues even better than a woman!" When Blind Lemon Jefferson emerged from the Deep Ellum scene in Dallas to deliver a raw guitar/vocal sound on Paramount Records in 1926, he knocked the piano-accompanied blues mamas out of fashion. Guitar-picked "country blues" was the new thing that everyone wanted to hear. Jefferson recorded more than eighty tracks, including the standards "Match Box Blues," "Long Lonesome Blues," "Black Snake Moan," and "See That My Grave's Kept Clean" before his body was found in a Chicago snowbank in December 1929.

The record business was dying at around the same time. The Stock Market Crash of October 1929 put the country into the Depression; who had seventy-five cents for a record? Commercial radio, which debuted in Pittsburgh in 1920, came of age during the bleak next decade, serving upbeat, escapist fare, so the labels had no market for authentic Southern poor-people music. Sales of 78RPM records in 1932 were just 6 percent of the total sold just three years earlier.

Dranes didn't put out another record after 1928, while Phillips's final session was in '29. The most popular of the trio, Johnson, last recorded in April 1930 in Atlanta, though his first two '78s were reissued on Vocalion in 1935.

You Don't Shake Hands with the Devil

Before Arizona Dranes, no one had ever made a gospel record that featured piano. And no label had yet released the raucous, sanctified sounds of the Pentecostal church to the new black music market. Dranes would be the first of her kind in June 1926.

She played "hot" piano and sang with her soul on fire at Roberts Temple Church of God in Christ on Fortieth Street in Chicago during her first recording visit. The Pentecostal "saints" were encouraged to let loose with their emotions, to become possessed by the Holy Ghost, but nobody'd ever seen anything quite like "Sister Arazoni." She came up from Texas with something to prove.

In the congregation was a street-corner mandolinist named Katie Bell Nubin and her eleven-year-old daughter Rosetta, who was already getting good on the guitar. A teenaged Sister Rosetta Tharpe became the Memphis Minnie of gospel music, then energized even more when electric guitar became available, greatly influencing Chuck Berry, among others. She recorded with electric guitar for the first time in 1941 on a revamp of Phillips's "Denomination Blues" she called "That's All." But Tharpe was almost stripped of her "Sister" rank by shocked churchgoers when she was backed by an eleven-piece jazz band and performed in secular venues. In the gospel field, you didn't cross over, you defected.

CHAPTER 2

From Slave Songs to Freedom Anthems

Dranes rarely played outside the church, and never in a club, but when gospel music became more of a business, religious acts had to sometimes play for the public to pay the bills. Clara Ward and the Ward Singers traded their choir robes for sequined gowns and took their act to Las Vegas in the '60s and never heard the end of it. When Aretha Franklin sang at her idol Ward's funeral in Philadelphia in 1973 someone murmured, "What's that blues singer doing up there?" Though they meet an hour before dawn, Saturday night and Sunday morning are polar opposites in the minds of many purists. But what is the gospel music of syncopated handclaps, thumping pianos, and wailing vocalists if not, simply, spiritualized secular music? Gospel's greatest songwriter Thomas A. Dorsey began his career as juke-joint piano player Georgia Tom.

Just as sinful businesses often reside next to storefront churches in predominantly black neighborhoods, gospel and blues have coexisted in tight quarters since they both grew out of spirituals. Some stations in the '40s and '50s, including fifty-thousand-watt WLAC in Nashville, aired them side by side. Many of the same independent labels that trafficked in R&B—including Aladdin, Peacock, Savoy, Vee-Jay, Specialty, and Excello—signed gospel acts as well.

Disregard the lyrics, and gospel is just an anointed step from rhythm and blues. But you can't diminish the importance of the words in these sermons set to music. The power, the rhythm, the incitement of great gospel music springs from lyrics of praise. The blues singer is all alone in this world, but the gospel singer is part of a family of faith.

Resistance to innovations in religious music goes back to the early 1700s, when a British pastor named Dr. Isaac Watts realized that the stodgy hymns of the day, taken straight from scripture and delivered at a plodding pace by a monotonous congregation, did not do justice to the Creator. To Watts, religious songs were a personal offering of praise and therefore should feature a more glorious presentation and heartfelt sentiment.

Updated ancient Protestant hymns—from "Amazing Grace" (by England's John Newton, though it's often credited to Dr. Watts) to "Oh Happy Day," a 1969 pop hit for the Edwin Hawkins Singers—make up much of the contemporary gospel songbook, but there's no way to overstate the influence of African American compositions of the 1800s. Slaves would hear stories of the Bible, but being unable to read, they would remember them by making work songs that we now call spirituals. While they couldn't sing openly about their own desire to be free, the original African Americans could rejoice in the story of Exodus, when the children of Israel yearned to be liberated from bondage. When slaves sang "Go down Moses, way down in Egypt land/ Tell old Pharaoh to let my people go," they did so with a vigor that suggests deep personal connection. Heavenly salvation and earthly freedom became intertwined. In the time of the Second Great Awakening (around 1790–1840), many slaves were converted to Christianity with the promise that great rewards awaited believers who endured great tribulations. They sang in the fields and envisioned better days.

My Soul Looks Back and Wonders

On an unseasonably breezy August afternoon in 1963, Dr. Martin Luther King Jr. was outside the Lincoln Memorial in Washington, DC, ready to give the speech of his life. But first there would be songs, untamed by social order, from a dignified African American queen who contorted her face, jerked her body, and chomped on lyrics as if a legacy of suffering flowed through her. Mahalia Jackson. Could any name better fit the physical and spiritual embodiment of Mother Church? Ma-HAIL-Yeah! There's a song in those syllables.

"How I got over," she began, softly. "Well, my soul looks back and wonders how I got over." Like most gospel performances, the song grew in intensity with each verse, and the crowd's response built from murmur to "Amen!" shouts. It took several minutes for the energized crowd of 250,000 to settle down; then Dr. King stepped up to the podium. "I have a dream," the civil rights leader intoned, "that one day on the red hills of Georgia, the sons of former slaves and the sons of former slave-owners will be able to sit together at the table of brotherhood."

It was appropriate that the freedom movement adopt as its soundtrack a style of music rooted in the African American struggle against oppression. "We Shall Overcome," an adaptation of Philadelphia reverend Charles A. Tindley's 1900 hymn "I'll Overcome, Some Day," was the anthem of the civil rights movement. Such gospel acts as the Staple Singers and Dorothy Love Coates were there with Dr. King in Birmingham in 1963, providing the soundtrack to the victorious campaign that forced the desegregation of Alabama's largest city and paved the way for the Civil Rights Act of 1964. "We are marching down Freedom Highway," Mavis Staples sang over her father's Delta blues guitar licks.

The '60s were a turning point in race relations in America, but the "long time coming'" of the 1964 Sam Cooke song "A Change Is Gonna Come" could refer not only to the passage of years it took for African Americans to finally approach the equal status guaranteed by the US Constitution, but for the rumbling rage of "Negro spirituals" to be expressed in public without a biblical veil.

Spirituals Find a Highbrow Champion

In the years directly following the Union victory in the Civil War, many newly free blacks discarded the "slave songs" as sad reminders. But internationally known Czech composer Antonin Dvořák, who was hired in 1892 as director of the National Conservatory of Music in New York City, was an unlikely patron of spirituals. Philanthropist Jeannette Thurber paid Dvořák $15,000 a year, an enormous sum back then, with the express purpose of creating a new, European-inspired school of American music.

One day, in the hall of the school on East Seventeenth Street, Dvořák heard a man with a deep baritone singing a spiritual. It was twenty-six-year-old African American student Harry T. Burleigh, who was on scholarship and did janitorial work to pay for room and board. Enchanted, Dvořák asked Burleigh to sing more songs from the fields of old, and the student did for more than an hour.

A few months later, the Czech composer wrote the article "The Real Value of Negro Melodies," in the *New York Herald*, which contended that "African Americans and Native Americans should be the foundation for the growth of American music. In the Negro melodies I discovered all that is needed for a great and noble school of music," he wrote. The upper crusties brought the famous classical composer to teach Americans to be more like Brahms and Wagner, and he saw the future in the music of slaves!

The uproar was immediate. "A truly American music based on the music of socially and politically marginal groups is ridiculous," wrote one of the top critics. But then came jazz and blues and funk and rock 'n' roll and hip-hop.

Less to do with the controversy than with a financial depression that depleted the Thurber fortune, Dvořák went back to Bohemia after three years in New York. Meanwhile, Burleigh became the most prominent arranger of spirituals, including "Swing Low Sweet Chariot," whose melody Dvořák incorporated into his famous "Symphony #9 in E Minor."

The "coon songs" of minstrelsy, which portrayed African Americans as either slow-witted or conniving, had been popular in the late 1800s. But Dvořák and Burleigh brought pride to the struggle, elevating spirituals from vaudeville spoofs to the concert stage. Post-slavery singing groups like Nashville's Fisk Jubilee Singers trained their voices to sing the cultured songs of European composers, but it was always "Down by the Riverside,"

"Ezekial Saw the Wheel," and the rest of the slave songs segment that brought the audience to its feet.

Blues music also sprang from the spirituals, with such desolate numbers as "Nobody Knows the Trouble I've Seen" and "Travelin' Shoes" laying the foundation for the lyrical realism that would be the domain of Southern bluesmen, including Lightnin' Hopkins and his lesser-known but equally influential cousin, Frankie Lee Sims of Marshall. There's also great release in the growling rhythms. Just as the slaves sang "The Lord Delivered Daniel (Why Not Me)" to hoist their spirits, blues singers shout about no-good liars and cheats as a way to get over them.

Though generally acknowledged as 1945–1960, the glory years of gospel can be traced to the 1920s, when a new crop of blues-based religious songs grew in popularity so quickly that the Baptist Church had to begrudgingly endorse them or lose parishioners to the more fervent Pentecostal services. After you heard Arizona Dranes on the piano or Blind Willie Johnson on the guitar, it was hard to get in the mood for "Bringing In the Sheaves." The people wanted the new fervency—jubilation, not assimilation—and eventually the bluesy gospel songs gained respectability and crossed denominational lines to become the preferred church music of most black Christians.

People have learned how to strum a guitar, but they don't have the soul. They don't feel it from the heart

CHAPTER 3

Washington Phillips

"The Height of Rural Originality"

The basin area between the Brazos and Trinity Rivers—fifty-two counties south of the Red River and north of San Antonio—were as fertile a spawning ground for blues pioneers as the Mississippi Delta, with Lemon Jefferson and his protégés Leadbelly, Lightnin' Hopkins, and T-Bone Walker all hailing from that region. Juke joint singers Bessie Tucker, Lillian Glinn, and Texas Alexander, plus bluesmen Frankie Lee Sims, Little Hat Jones, J. T. "Funny Papa" Smith, Lil' Son Jackson, and Smokey Hogg also grew up in the "Black Waxy Prairie" towns. And let's not forget the Soul Stirrers from Trinity, who revolutionized gospel quartet singing long before Sam Cooke joined the group in 1950.

Dranes from Sherman, Phillips from Teague, and Temple's Johnson all grew up in and around this blackland cradle of the blues, where music and work went hand in hand. It was cotton country, yielding about two million bales a year (one-sixth of the entire US production) at its peak in the early 1900s.

You had to eat, and so the fields were full of pickers. But the back-breaking work also provided an incentive to become another kind of picker. The goal was to play music so well that folks would give you money to hear it. That was making it! If you were blind, you couldn't work in the fields, so your choices were musician or beggar. But what sometimes starts as a way to make a living becomes a way of life.

Washington Phillips was a farmer and a preacher and a musician in equal parts. His sweetly sung gospel folk tunes, bathed in a celestial haze of notes from an instrument that sounds like a child's music box, were simple prayers. But his ethereal sound was also highly developed to the point of being almost psychedelic. From what background did this starkly original artist emerge fully formed?

His grandfather, also named Washington Phillips, was a slave, born in Kentucky in 1801 and most likely "sold down the river" to a Texas landowner in the 1850s, along with his wife Ann and teenaged sons Austin, Houston, and

Tim. Not long after they were emancipated on "Juneteenth," June 19, 1865, the Phillips men started buying farmland in the freedmen's community of Simsboro, about eighty miles southeast of Dallas.

Both Tim and Houston Phillips had sons they named after their father, who lived to be eighty-one. The oldest grandson, Tim's boy "Little Wash," was born in 1880 and went on to record for Columbia Records from 1927 to 1929.

Houston's son Washington Phillips, born in 1891, was a farmer who went crazy and, in 1930, was committed to the Texas State Hospital in Austin, where he died eight years later.

When the haunting spirituals of Washington Phillips were first made available on CD in 1991 with *I Am Born To Preach the Gospel* (Yazoo), the liner notes incorrectly based biographical information on the death certificate of the cousin who died in the state asylum at age forty-seven. The Washington Phillips who recorded such distinctive gospel tunes as "Lift Him Up, That's All," "What Are They Doing in Heaven Today?" and "Paul and Silas In Jail" lived until 1954, when he died at age seventy-four after a fall down the stairs at the city hall in Teague, the nearest town to Simsboro.

I stumbled upon this case of mistaken identity in 2002 when I was a music critic for the *Austin American-Statesman* and used the Austin death of the "wrong" Washington Phillips as a local connection that would justify a lengthy profile of an intriguing gospel obscurity.

Another bit of misinformation passed on was that Phillips backed himself on a dolceola, a rare "portable grand piano" produced only from 1903 to 1908 in Toledo, Ohio. What a weird tale this was, a preacher with a head full of voices playing heavenly tunes on a doomed miniature keyboard!

But the dolceola theory was also shot down, once and for all, by an article I recently discovered which ran in the *Teague Chronicle* in November 1907. Under the headline "A Unique Instrument," the brief detailed "a negro in town, named George Washington Phillips," who played music from "a box about 2 X 3 feet, 6 inches deep, and which he has strung violin strings, something on the order of an autoharp . . . He uses both hands and plays all sorts of airs." The twenty-seven-year-old Phillips called his homemade instrument a "Manzarene," the article said. East Texas had never seen or heard anything like Washington Phillips, who dropped the "George" as his grandfather and cousin did. Sixty-five years after his death, the world still hasn't heard anything like those tracks Phillips recorded into a single mic in a makeshift Dallas studio.

A UNIQUE INSTRUMENT

There is a negro in town, named George Washington PHILLIPS, who has manufactured one of the most unique musical instrument we ever saw. It is a box about 2 X 3 feet, 6 inches deep, an which he has strung violin strings, something on the order of an autoharp. He is as black as the ace of spades, but the music he gets out of that roughly made box is certainly surprising. He uses both hands and plays all sorts of airs. He calls it a "Manzarene." The tricks which nature plays are stranger than fiction.

"I Want to Tell You the Natural Fact"

Wash Phillips was a product of post-slavery black America, when blues and gospel music were an ocean apart. Not only were blacks separate from whites, they were also divided amongst each other as sinners and saints. Then once again in church, split between the mainstream Baptist and Methodist denominations and the screaming, pounding "holy rollers" of the Pentecostal sect. But Phillips, an unordained "jackleg" preacher, wasn't made for those categorical times. "He was just so different from everyone else," said Doris Foreman Nealy, who grew up in Simsboro next to the Phillips farm. As a younger man, Wash Phillips would roam Freestone County on Sundays to sing and testify at Pentecostal and African Methodist Episcopal services. But later in his life he settled into his role as Rev. Wash Phillips at the Pleasant Hill Missionary Baptist Church, just down the road from his farm. "He was an enlightened person," his second cousin Earl Phillips said in 2002, recalling that the singing farmer/preacher smelled of liniment oil and made herbal remedies that he sold from his mule cart, along with plums and ribbon cane syrup.

He sang and played hymns and originals on his customized zithers until the very end, his former Simsboro neighbors recall, but none of the half dozen I interviewed in 2002 knew he ever made records.

Washington Phillips might've been almost completely forgotten if his career didn't receive a posthumous jolt in the 1970s, with Ry Cooder covering "Denomination Blues" on 1972's *Into the Purple Valley* and then reworking "You Can't Stop a Tattler" on '74's *Paradise and Lunch*. Renamed "Tattler," with Phillips sharing writing credits with Cooder and producer Russ Titelman, that's the arrangement Linda Ronstadt used on her platinum-selling *Hasten Down the Wind* LP. Royalties never rolled his way, because no one knew anything about this Washington Phillips, who could've come from anywhere.

When the *Teague Chronicle* ran an article about Phillips's death on September 20, 1954, there was mention of the mule cart, but not the musical career. They didn't even get his name or age right, calling him Wash Williams, 77.

"He knew he had talent, but he was just ol' Wash Phillips," said his second cousin Virgil Keeton. "Don't nobody get famous from Teague."

"I Had a Good Father and Mother"

Washington Phillips, the singer and zitherist, was born January 11, 1880, the sixth child of Tim Phillips (b. Kentucky 1843) and Nancy Cooper Phillips (b. Tennessee 1848), who were married in 1867. The family lived on a farm in Simsboro next to patriarch Washington's spread, land whose ownership can be traced to Dr. James Wills, the great-granduncle of Western swing king Bob Wills (born in nearby Kosse). According to deed documents kept at the Freestone county clerk's office in Fairfield, James Wills sold "Abstract 217" in 1854 to H. M. Ewing, who sold it to James McMillan just before the Civil War.

In 1870, Tim and Houston went in together on 320 acres, purchased for $240 from neighbor McMillan, head of one of the last few white families in Simsboro. Their older brother Austin (b. 1838) and wife Drucilla bought their first parcel in 1867 and accumulated 203 acres over the next two decades. Land was freedom to the former slaves.

After Tim Phillips died of pneumonia in 1911 at age sixty-eight, his eighty-seven-acre spread was split equally between his youngest sons Wash, Dock, and Tim, according to property tax records. Their mother Nancy and Wash's first wife Anna, whom he married in 1915, were also listed as owners when the Phillips family signed an oil, gas, and mineral rights lease in 1919 that granted them one-eighth commission on any natural resources found on the property. The deal must not have yielded much money because Wash's younger brothers soon cut out on their own, with Tim Jr. listed in the 1927 Mexia city directory as working for a brick company and married to a woman named Jeffie. Dock headed up to Canada, according to family historian Earl Phillips, where there was work laying railroad tracks.

It's not known if the 1922 Kirvin race riots, following the murder and mutilation of a seventeen-year-old white girl, also played a role in the younger Phillips brothers' exit from Freestone County. As detailed in the Monty Akers book *Flames After Midnight*, black field hand Snapp Curry, whose ex-wife said she saw him with blood on his clothes, allegedly confessed and implicated two other black men in the murder of the teenager. All three were doused with gasoline and burned to death, while a fourth man was lynched. Amid fears of retaliation, a white militia from Kirvin, nine miles away, rode into Simsboro and tried to take into custody Allie and Leroy Gibson for unspecified charges. When the brothers resisted, they were shot to death, as were two whites in return fire, which enflamed racial tensions so badly that the Texas Rangers were called in to defuse the situation. The threat of an uprising made national news, with one wire story describing "blacks in open revolt against the whites." The acrimony lasted for years, said Doris Foreman Nealy, whose mother was a Gibson. But it also brought Simsboro's black community closer together.

Prejudice has long been the soot of Freestone County, where slaves surpassed the

number of whites, about 3,600 to 3,200, in 1860. From 1850 to 1860, the slave population of Texas grew from 58,161 to 182,556, as white planters fled south and west to keep their slaves from deserting and joining the Union Army.

Up from Slavery

The family took the Phillips name from the plantation they worked on, according to an eighty-five-year-old Earl Phillips, the grandson of Austin and Drucilla. I interviewed Earl by phone in Denver in 2002, but like so many elderly witnesses from years ago, he's passed on since. But he wrote down the family history as it was told to him, and his second cousin Wardell Phillips has a copy. Earl Phillips's document says his great-grandfather Washington Phillips was owned by the men named Karner and Phillips, who founded Mexia's Karner-Phillips department store. But I originally dismissed that info because Karner-Phillips wasn't established until 1878. There were a few bits of Earl's family history disputed by public records, so everything had to be independently verified.

The 1860 Slave Schedules for Freestone County, however, shows that a John Karner owned slaves whose ages (names weren't listed) roughly matched the elder Washington Phillips (sixty), his wife Ann (forty-five), sons Houston (twenty) and Tim (seventeen), and daughters Katy (twelve) and Susan (six). Patriarch Phillips was actually fifty-nine and Houston nineteen, but it wasn't uncommon for census takers of the time to round up ages, especially for African Americans, who often didn't know their own birthdays.

The 1880 census shows the Phillips family was from Kentucky, a state known for "stocking and raising" slaves for sale after the transatlantic slave trade was discontinued in 1808. This may or may not have had something to do with the Appalachian touches of the Wash Phillips instrumentation. Religious "camp meetings" were especially popular among both blacks and whites in Kentucky and Tennessee during the time the gospel singer's grandparents were coming of age in the early 1800s. But any link is pure conjecture, which is sometimes all we have this many years later.

A native of Bavaria, Karner stowed away to the land of opportunity as a teenager and fought with Sam Houston at the Battle of San Jacinto, which brought Texas independence in 1836. Later, known as "Dutch John the Indian Fighter," Karner was given land for his deeds and bought up parcels around his grant—sixty-five properties in all—in the 1850s. Some of his dealings were with a man named Frank A. Phillips, who may have owned the plantation Earl Phillips told me about, but I was unable to find any other information to back that up. An 1860 county agricultural report said there were seven plantations of over five hundred acres in Freestone County, where cotton was king and corn was queen.

When the Civil War broke out and Freestone County voted 585-3 to secede from the Union, Karner joined the Confederate army. He came home in 1865 to empty slave quarters.

"Juneteenth was always a big day for Wash Phillips," said Nealy, a retired nursing school instructor, who found the second-known photo of Phillips, fronting his mules in his Sunday's best, circa 1950. "He'd dig a pit and slaughter a hog and cook it all day."

The Juneteenth celebration was held in the grassy picnic area common to all three black churches in Simsboro. They were Hogie Primitive Baptist, Wesley Tabernacle A.M.E., and Pleasant Hill Missionary Baptist—and Phillips was acquainted with the pulpits at all three. He also loved to stir up the congregation at the "sanctified" St. Paul Church of God in Christ in Teague, according to May Nella Palmore, who was eighty-two in 2002. "His singing really fit with that crowd," she said of the denomination that believed in soul possession as the only true evidence of baptism. "He had such a strong, powerful voice."

His occupation was listed as "holiness minister" in the 1930 census, when he was living in Dallas, but Wash Phillips may have been devoted to that view of entire sanctification, or "Christian perfection," in the early 1900s. Naming his instrument a "Manzarene" could have been inspired by the Pentecostal Church of the Nazarene, a Los Angeles offshoot of Methodism, which formed in 1895 and moved its headquarters to Texas soon after. The church newspaper, the *Nazarene Messenger*, was published in Grayson County, where Wash's older brothers Felix and Fletcher and sister Mattie had moved by 1900. It was in the nearby town of Pilot Point in 1908 that the Independent Holiness Church merged with the Pentecostal Nazarene group to form The Church of the Nazarene, now based in Kansas City, with more than two million followers worldwide.

The Houston and Texas Central Railway, which had a station in Mexia (where Wash worked as a waiter in 1900) and a terminus in the Grayson County seat of Sherman, made travel between the two places easy. It's quite possible Phillips spent a lot of time in Sherman with his older siblings, and, if so, he'd certainly heard the name "Nazarene" around the time he was making his box of angelic strings.

"Sacred Porch Songs"

Washington Phillips recorded eighteen sides for Columbia in five sessions in Dallas, from December 1927 to December 1929. His first three '78s—all released in 1928—registered his best sales, topping off with 8,725 copies of the debut "Take Your Burden To the Lord and Leave It There" b/w "Lift Him Up That's All." The follow-up single "Denomination Blues" was released on July 30, 1928, and sold about 6,625 copies, according to Columbia order records. The third '78, "Paul and Silas in Jail" b/w "A Mother's Last Word to Her Son," released November 20, 1928, sold about 5,600 copies.

FOUR RACE ARTISTS SIGNED FOR COLUMBIA

Four new race artists were signed to record exclusively for the Columbia Phonograph Company during the recent Southern trip of Frank Walker, executive in Columbia's recording studios.

Blind Willie Johnson is reported as a new sensation in the South in singing sacred songs to a fine guitar accompaniment of his own.

Lillian Glinn is a new singer of blues, full of pep and personality. She possesses an extraordinary voice, of which every word gets over on the phonograph.

Washington Phillips presents gospel records that are different. His songs are admired for the significant meaning he gives them, and he accompanies himself on an instrument never before heard.

Laughing Charley is the latest addition of race contributions to the "Joy Note" in living. He sings blues with a laugh.

The first releases of all these artists have just been listed for Columbia's next monthly supplement of race records.

But after the Depression hit, record sales tanked. Phillips's seventh and final '78, "The Church Needs Good Deacons" b/w "I Had a Good Father and Mother," released in December 1930, sold fewer than one thousand copies. Forty-seven when he made his first recordings, Phillips had completely recessed into the rural life by age fifty. He never received a penny for his records, with the session cards denoting them as "non-royalty."

There's too much talent and originality in Phillips's music for it not to eventually find an audience, and what Cooder revived continues to grow slowly. A swell in interest in the zither-playing preacher came when his song "Mother's Last Word to Her Son" wove a spiritual thread through *We Need to Talk About Kevin*, the 2011 Tilda Swinton film about a school massacre. Covers of Phillips songs by the likes of Vince Gill, Mogwai, Phish, Ralph Stanley, Gillian Welch, Rodney Crowell, and Mavis Staples continue to bring attention, while many more musicians are content to listen and be inspired by the true artist who created against all odds.

"I've just become fascinated with the bizarre world he invented for himself," said Chicago lo-fi musician Owen Ashworth, who recorded an EP of Phillips covers as Advance Base. "The way his voice blends with the music is so hypnotic and kinda lonely and openhearted. There's such an effort to connect."

Calling the music of Washington Phillips "the absolute height of rural originality," Gary Harrison wrote in his fretlesszithers.com blog in 2005 that, "It would have been unusual enough if he had merely acquired and learned to play a fretless zither, an instrument with virtually no known performance tradition. But it appears that what (Phillips) did was to re-configure two fretless zithers, to expand the range of both the melody and accompaniment sections . . . and then to become a highly skilled player on his creation, producing other-worldly tones unlike those made by any other instrument." While playing two zithers simultaneously, one hand for the chords and one hand for the melody, this self-made virtuoso also sang in a vulnerable, penetrating voice of faith.

Wash Phillips created sacred porch songs that point to a higher power, for how could man alone create music for the angels?

The Man from New York

It's safe to say that if Columbia Records talent scout/producer Frank B. Walker and his engineer ("Freiberg" on session notes) didn't make yearly recording trips to Dallas from '27 to '29, the musical gifts of Washington Phillips might've never escaped East Texas. Unlike Blind Willie Johnson, who performed all over the state and up the Eastern Seaboard, Phillips didn't rely on music for his livelihood, so he rarely drifted far from Freestone County. Even after his records were released, there's no evidence he ever played a concert.

Talent scouts from the North usually ran ads in African American newspapers telling when and where regional auditions would take place, but they also consulted locals in the know. These label reps were coming all the way from New York or Chicago to hear the very best.

Though Phillips's parents were illiterate, he had a fourth-grade education and could read. But copies of the *Dallas Express* and *Houston Informer* didn't make it to Simsboro, isolated from post-Reconstruction society by design. Wash Phillips most likely came to the attention of Columbia through his association with blues guitarist Blind Lemon Jefferson, who had become a national star for Paramount Records a year earlier with "Long Lonesome Blues." Jefferson (b. 1894) also grew up on a farm in Freestone County, and played fish fries and house parties with Wash and the younger Phillips brothers Dock and Tim. That information came from a 1998 interview with 106-year-old Charlie Hurd, a former Jefferson running buddy, in the book *Deep Ellum: The Other Side of Dallas* by Alan Govenar and Jay Brakefield. Jefferson had beat Phillips to the studio by two years with the spiritual single "I Want to Be Like Jesus in My Heart" b/w "All I Want is That Pure Religion," recorded under the pseudonym Deacon L. J. Bates.

Though Wash Phillips, according to neighbor Durden Dixon, sang secular songs about fishing, boll weevils, and such on his porch and wagon, he recorded only gospel songs, though his moralistic lyrics often bit like the blues. Genre didn't matter to Walker, whose search for the most soulful musicians found blues superstar Bessie Smith in Alabama and blind guitarist Riley Puckett and fiddler Gid Tanner in Georgia. Columbia forged the "hillbilly music" market with the 15000-D series ("Familiar Tunes—Old and New"), which had a big hit with "Don't Let Your Deal Go Down" by Charlie Poole and the North Carolina Ramblers in 1925, almost two years before Ralph Peer discovered Jimmie Rodgers and the Carter Family in Bristol, Tennessee.

Frank Walker left Columbia in 1932, just two years before it was sold to American Recording Company for a mere $70,000, to became head of RCA Victor. During eleven years with RCA, Walker supervised landmark jazz and Big Band recordings, including "Body and Soul" by Coleman Hawkins, "In the Mood" by the Glenn Miller Orchestra in 1939, and "Take the 'A' Train" by Duke Ellington in '41. Financially set after twenty-five years as a record exec, Walker retired in 1944 but was coaxed back two years later to help launch MGM Records, where he signed and mentored a new country singer named Hank Williams. Although his name is not well known, Walker's been called "The Dean of the American Record Industry," and yet he might've gone back to banking if not for a chance encounter on a Manhattan street corner in 1919.

In a 1962 interview with Mike Seeger, Walker recalled that he was thirty years old, just back from WWI, when he ran into his former Navy commander Francis S. Whited. When Walker said he was looking for a job, Whited offered him one as his assistant at Columbia. "But I don't know anything about the phonograph business," Walker said. "Neither do I," said Whited, whose family, the Du Ponts, were heavy investors in the Columbia Phonograph and Dictaphone Company at the time. Walker learned all the intricacies of making records at the label's plant in Bridgeport, Connecticut, and eventually worked his way up as an artists and repertoire executive.

For the first week of three Decembers in a row, starting in 1927, Walker and Freiberg set up a studio in Dallas and recorded dozens of acts at each session. Phillips most likely came to the city on the Trinity and Brazos Valley Railway, sixteen stops from Teague to Dallas. "These people would show up, sometimes from eight or nine hundred miles away. How they got there I'll never know," Walker told Seeger. "They never asked you for money. . . . They had just made a phonograph record, and to them that was the next best thing to being the President of the United States."

What he remembered most about Washington Phillips was his "novelty accompaniment," as his instrument was described on the label credits. "It was something he made himself," Walker said in 1962. "Nobody on earth could use it but him."

When Columbia came to Texas looking for talent, it was twenty years after Phillips had been featured in the article in the *Teague Chronicle* that marveled at his instrumental prowess. When his name was called in Dallas, Ol' Wash and his Manzarene were ready.

Dallas in December: the Sessions

Phillips recorded four titles on Friday, December 2, 1927—two originals and two covers. Philadelphia hymn writer Charles A. Tindley's "Take Your Burden to the Lord and Leave It There" was recorded a year earlier by Blind Joe Taggart for Vocalion, but Phillips probably first heard it in church. "Lift Him Up That's All," another hymnal mainstay, is sometimes incorrectly credited to prolific Protestant songwriter Johnson Oatman Jr., but only the title is in common with Phillips's version.

On Saturday, Blind Willie Johnson came up from Marlin to nail six tracks, including the future classics "If I Had My Way," "Motherless Children," "Nobody's Fault But Mine," and "Dark Was the Night (Cold Was the Ground)." December 3, 1927, was one of the most remarkable days in Texas recording history.

But December 2 and 5 weren't too bad, either. Phillips was called back on Monday and recorded his most famous song "Denomination Blues" in two parts. With Wash's magical musical contraption and Blind Willie taking slide guitar where it had never been before, Walker must've thought Texas was the most brilliantly weird and musically adventurous place on earth.

Other acts who recorded at that first Dallas session were Lillian Glinn, backed by Willie Tyson on piano, mandolinist Coley Jones and the Dallas String Band, blues singers William McCoy, Hattie Hudson, and Gertrude Perkins, plus Billiken Johnson, whose popular Deep Ellum act consisted of train impersonations ("Interurban Blues") and other sound effects. Walker told Seeger that the acts auditioned in the morning, rehearsed in the afternoon, and recorded in the evening.

It's not known, for fact, where these historic December 1927 recordings took place. The East Coast record men, who made frequent trips to Dallas, Memphis, New Orleans, and Atlanta from 1927 to 1930, sometimes set up their makeshift studios in hotels. But because Walker and Freiberg were using the new "Viva-Tonal!" recording process, licensed from Western Electric, those first sessions probably took place in the Columbia Records complex, which covered three storefronts (2000–2004) on North Lamar Street in Dallas's West End. The building was torn down long ago.

When Phillips's debut of "Burden"/ "Lift" hit stores in January 1928, Columbia ran an ad in black newspapers trumpeting "A new type of gospel recording—a great singer and songs full of longing and accompanied by an instrument never before seen." The ad in the January 14 *Louisiana Weekly* included a photo of Washington Phillips holding two restrung zithers that appeared to be attached to each other.

On Walker's next swing through Dallas, the first week of December 1928, Phillips recorded four songs with spoken intros, perhaps at the urging of Walker, who had a big hit in 1926 with "Death's Black Train Is Coming" by Atlanta Rev. J. M. Gates. Or it could be that, after returning to Freestone County as a moderately successful recording artist in early 1928, the preacher had become more in demand and therefore more confident in his sermonizing. On December 4, 1928, he laid down "I Am Born to Preach the Gospel" and "Train Your Child," the latter with a long instrumental passage that says as much about discipline as the words. The next day Phillips followed "Blind Texas Marlin" (Blind Willie in blues disguise?) into the studio with Tindley's "What Are They Doing In Heaven Today?" and "Jesus Is My Friend," a reworking of the 1860's standard "What a Friend We Have in Jesus."

For his final recording session, December 2, 1929, in Dallas, Phillips did away with the preacher poetry and recorded eight all-musical tracks—only four of which were released on 78s. The Dranes cover, "Mother's Last Word to Her Daughter" b/w "I've Got the Key to the Kingdom," were followed by Phillips originals, "The Church Needs New Deacons" b/w "I Had a Good Father and Mother."

Of the four other tracks recorded at the session and not released by Columbia, the masters to "You Can't Stop a Tattler," parts one and two, were eventually found and first issued in a 1968 gospel blues compilation entitled *This Old World's in a Hell of a Fix* (Biograph). Since "Tattler, Part 1" is not really a gospel song but more of a moralistic marriage ditty, it was probably not originally released because gospel singers didn't put out secular music back then. Another two-part Phillips song, "The World Is in a Bad Fix Everywhere," has not only never been released, it cannot be found in the Sony vaults. The label has index cards from the session that show "Bad Fix" was recorded December 2, 1929, in two takes.

A Career Stalls, a Cousin Crashes

After his recording debut, a recently divorced Phillips moved to Dallas for a spell, perhaps to be closer to the music business. A fellow boarder in the house on Lotus Street in Oak Cliff was forty-two-year-old Susie Miles, a native of Mississippi, who would become the second Mrs. Washington Phillips in 1934. Wash Phillips's dreams of being a successful recording artist were over by that time, and he and Susie settled in Simsboro.

His cousin, Houston's son Wash Phillips, was no longer around when the singer returned. According to confidential medical records, which a Texas State Hospital official read to me over the phone under the condition his name not be used, the Washington Phillips who was eleven years younger and died

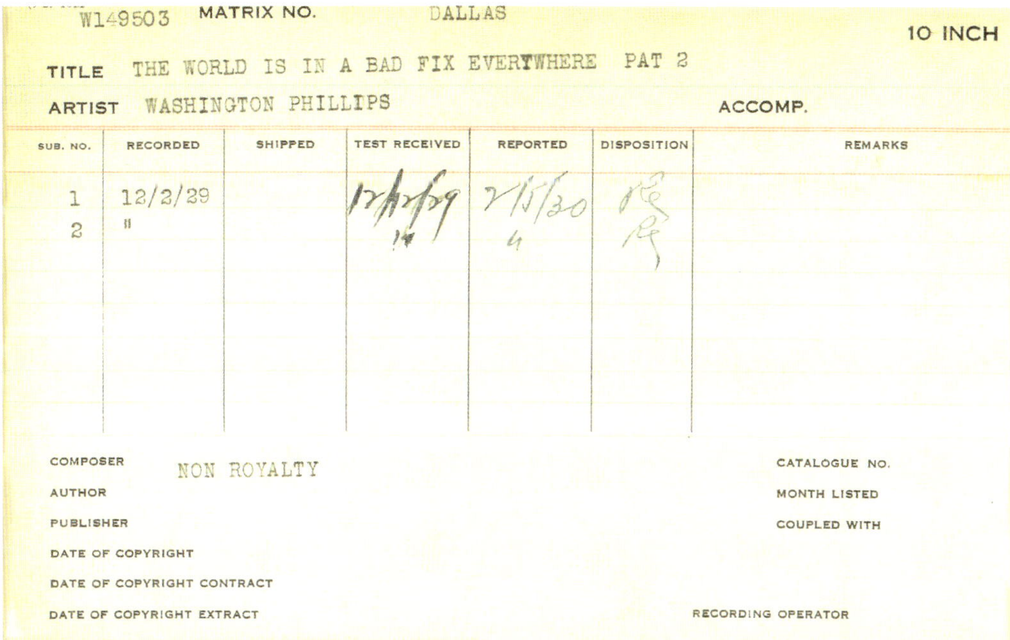
W149503 MATRIX NO. DALLAS

10 INCH

TITLE THE WORLD IS IN A BAD FIX EVERYWHERE PAT 2

ARTIST WASHINGTON PHILLIPS ACCOMP.

SUB. NO.	RECORDED	SHIPPED	TEST RECEIVED	REPORTED	DISPOSITION	REMARKS
1	12/2/29		12/12/29	2/15/30		
2	"		14	4		

COMPOSER NON ROYALTY

AUTHOR

PUBLISHER

DATE OF COPYRIGHT

DATE OF COPYRIGHT CONTRACT

DATE OF COPYRIGHT EXTRACT

CATALOGUE NO.

MONTH LISTED

COUPLED WITH

RECORDING OPERATOR

sixteen years earlier, was a prosperous farmer and a good husband and father to wife Elector and eight children until 1929, when he started suffering from paranoid delusions. Following a land dispute with his brothers, this Wash Phillips built a fence around his house, lived in a crawlspace, and heard voices from God telling him not to work. As his family was forced to survive on parched corn and other scraps, a judge had this Phillips committed to the Austin sanitarium. The Washington Phillips who was originally credited as the gospel pioneer died there of tuberculosis on New Year's Eve, 1938.

Though the musician Wash Phillips was married three times that we know of, there's no record that he had children, but former neighbor Loycie Mims says a man claiming to be the son of Wash Phillips and first wife Anna Harrison showed up at the funeral in 1954. "But then he was gone as quick as he came, and we never saw him again." The Phillips farm went to his last wife Aurelia, but she sold it to Wash's first cousin and best friend Eldon Phillips. Eldon's son Wardell Phillips currently owns the land, which he uses to raise cattle and hogs.

Debunking the Dolceola

The label on Washington Phillips's first '78s credited a "novelty accomp." for the flowing instrumentation. Later, British music historian Paul Oliver, who was compiling a companion album to his book *Screening the Blue*s, found Columbia notes that described the instrument this strange and gentle holy man played as a "dulceola," which may have been a variation on dulcimer. When Dutch label Agram put out the first full album of 1920s Phillips recordings in 1979, the instrument pictured on the cover was a hammered dulcimer.

Musicologists Roger Misiewicz from Canada and Pat Conte of New York independently discovered the dolceola in 1983, and when they studied the sound of this keyboard-activated board zither, they believed they had solved the mystery of how Phillips got that ethereal sound. Agram proudly announced, in the notes of a 1984 compilation, that Phillips had played a dolceola on his recordings, and that rather arbitrary determination became fact to most Washington Phillips enthusiasts.

It's not the first time a legend was built on a myth. But even after New Orleans researcher

Lynn Abbott found, in 1984, the January 1928 ad in *Louisiana Weekly* that showed Phillips sitting behind two zithers, many clung to the Dutch theory, especially after Wash champion Ry Cooder used a dolceola on the 1986 *Crossroads* soundtrack to approximate the Phillips sound. "The only reason anybody even cares about the dolceola today is because of Washington Phillips," Memphis musician Andy Cohen, one of fewer than forty dolceola owners in the world, said in 2002.

But when I talked to townspeople who actually saw Phillips play, they all described a plucking motion, not pressing down keys. "It was a boxlike instrument he made from the insides of a piano," said Durden Dixon, who was born in 1940 and therefore was fourteen when the old man died. Mr. Wash was "kind of a hermit" who shooed the neighborhood boys away from his dewberry bushes, Dixon recalled. But sometimes he'd call 'em up to the porch and play them some songs on his strange harp-like instrument.

Virgil Keeton demonstrated the playing style as a dance of the thumb and forefinger on strings. It's obvious from the photo following the first recording session that Phillips played Phonoharp zithers, not homemade ones. But the 1907 article, as well as several witnesses I talked to, describe a "box-like" instrument. Perhaps Phillips kept his zithers in a wooden box for resonating and carrying purposes, but then took them out for the posed photo?

"It's just crazy," said Yazoo honcho Richard Nevins. "My ears are telling me that he's plucking the strings. It sounds like a zither to me. Then, lo and behold, along comes that picture of him holding the zithers in the studio and some people are still saying he played a dolceola!"

Gregg Miner is one dolceola owner who had to admit that he was naïve to ignore the 1928 photo. After the 2002 *Austin American-Statesman* article revealed the mistaken identity and dispelled the dolceola theory, Miner and fellow musicologists Kelly Williams and Gary Harrison did extensive research into the instrumentation of Washington Phillips. All three came away 100 percent sure that he didn't play a dolceola, but a common zither, albeit one with self-invented stringing and a unique tuning pattern. "It is impossible to duplicate or approach the sounds Phillips makes on a dolceola," Miner wrote on his www.minermusic.com web site in 2003. "Happily for the legend, it is also all but impossible for any of us to duplicate his self-styled virtuoso techniques on a Phonoharp-type zither!"

Fretless zithers and celestaphones, the two stringed instruments Phillips is believed to be holding in the 1928 photo, are normally played with a melody section of two octaves of C. Phillips's songs are in the key of F and span a melody range of three octaves. Musicologists marvel at Phillips's inventive instrumentation, but let's not forget that he had at least twenty years to tinker with his Manzarene before the men from New York came down with their record-making machines. Time and solitude and a night sky full of stars. His log cabin in the middle of nowhere provided a perfect rehearsal space and no doubt inspired the expansive tendencies of the Phillips sound.

I Am Born to Preach the Gospel and I Sure Do Love My Job

That Phillips was well-versed in the varying beliefs and customs of different churches is evident in "Denomination Blues," the song that built his bond with the counterculture. Coyly denouncing hypocrisy in organized religion, Phillips mocks six different black denominations before launching into the verse: "You can go to college, you can go to school/ But if you ain't got Jesus, you a educated fool." On the second part of "Denomination," Phillips hits harder, singing of preachers who "think they're doing well" and that "all they want is your money and you can go to hell."

That theme of religious insincerity carried over to another Phillips original, "The Church Needs Good Deacons," with its lines about church leaders running around on their wives. The lyrical bitterness was perhaps born from too many Sundays waiting to be called to the pulpit while less pious men with degrees spewed their pretentious babble.

"He was a good church man," recalled Darnell Nelms, who grew up in Simsboro. "But he was so peculiar. Miss Susie was such a nice, soft-spoken gal, and they seemed like an odd couple." Mr. Wash was the gregarious preacher-peddler, plucking a Jews harp down the dirt road and practicing his sermons when he didn't know anyone was listening. And then he had that contraption that he'd set on the table at church and strum that spooky music. "We thought he was the boogeyman," laughed Nealy's sister Mary Foreman.

By the late '40s, when Pleasant Hill bestowed the "Reverend" title on Phillips, his jackleg days were over and he became a one-church preacher. Pleasant Hill still has some of the old Sunday school journals, going back almost seventy years. His third wife, Sister Aurelia (Simpson), whom he married in 1950, two years after Susie died of a stroke at seventy, was the Sunday school teacher. One entry from 1952 notes that "the house was called to order by singing 'There Is a Fountain Filled with Blood' led by Rev. Wash Phillips." A preacher to the end.

"Even though he was up there in age, it shocked us all when Wash Phillips died," said Nealy, who was away at college at the time. "He seemed like the kind of person that was going to live forever."

A mighty spirit left the Simsboro community in September 1954.

"Leave it there, oh leave it there," he sang in that sweet tenor of the truth. "Take your burden to the lord and leave it there." Sometimes it can be as simple as that, knowing when and where to let go. Sometimes sixteen tracks is the whole shot.

Who was Washington Phillips, a musician so obscure they initially gave all the credit to his cousin? Having burnt a week in 2002 tracking down information on the Washington Phillips who died in Austin in 1938, I became skeptical of any new details. Which Washington Phillips were they talking about? For instance, I found Annie Mae Flewellen, related to both grandsons named Washington Phillips, in California, and when she recounted an episode where Wash Phillips, the gospel singer, gave her a pinch of snuff when she was small ("I just went to the floor," she said. "Passed out cold"), I tried to correct her. That must've been your first cousin, married to Elector, I said. "Uh, uh," Flewellen said, firmly. "It was the Wash

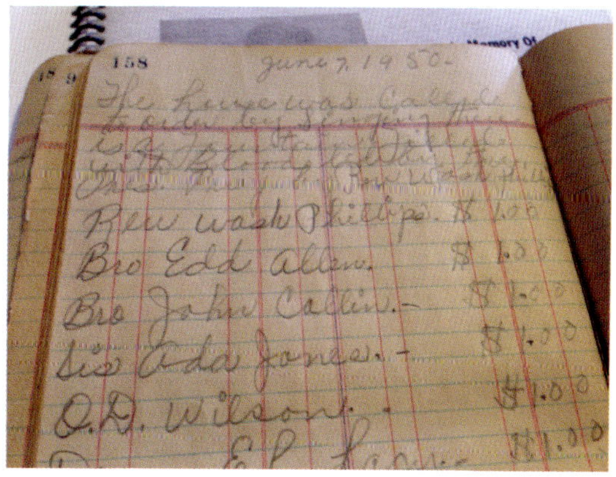

Phillips from Simsboro." That didn't sound like the Bible-thumper who preached good parenting in "Train Your Child."

When Durden Dixon took me to Wash Phillips's land that first time, I was looking around where the house used to sit and amid all these old pieces of tin and rusted buckets, there was a little brown bottle, half-buried. When I picked it up, emptied the dirt and showed Dixon, he laughed. "That's his snuff bottle, man." The next day an appraiser at Rue's Antiques in Austin confirmed that the bottle once held Garrett's snuff circa the early '50s. What do you know, Annie Mae Flewellen's seventy-four-year-old memory was on the mark.

If there's anything this story has told me, it's that sometimes what's true and what's false comes from where you least expect it. The search is the destination.

The three men named George Washington Phillips—the grandfather from Kentucky and his grandsons from Freestone County—are buried in the Cotton Gin Cemetery in the countryside six miles west of Teague. But several searches of the "colored" side could locate only two tombstones. That the Washington Phillips who was gospel's great disappearing act would take his eternal rest in an unmarked grave seems about par for this course in music history.

The great musician didn't die in the state asylum. And his instrument was not a dolceola. It never really mattered what he played—it doesn't change the music he left behind. But it's comforting to know that the singer who has affected so few people so profoundly didn't live out his last few years in mental torment but surrounded by the people who knew and respected him for who he was.

CHAPTER 4

Arizona Dranes

"Filled My Soul with the Holy Ghost"

When Arizona Dranes, blind and broke and a little wary, took a train from Fort Worth in June 1926 to record for OKeh Records, there was no assurance that anything would come out of the trip. "Please understand that we are bringing you to Chicago to make test records first," a rep for OKeh wrote when he sent travel arrangements. "We do not guarantee to release them for sale."

Whatever trepidation OKeh might've had evaporated on June 17, 1926, when Dranes sat at the piano and, with six songs recorded that day, created a spirit/flesh communion that would later be known as "the gospel beat." Her locomotive hands drove each other, with the percussive left—the rhythm section—dancing on and around the beat like a jazz bassist. This drawling church lady from Texas was playing barrelhouse piano! But her piercing, otherwordly voice and lyrics of deep praise were so filled with the Holy Spirit that the music was undeniably Christian.

A singer sits at the piano and loses all inhibitions while being in complete control of the instrument: Little Richard, Ray Charles, Jerry Lee Lewis, etc. Arizona Dranes started all that in 1926 with six "test records" that have stood the test of time.

The first musical star of the Church of God in Christ (COGIC), the Pentecostal denomination that brought instruments, dancing, and polyrhythmic handclaps to the black church, Dranes is strangely unknown today except to small baskets of admiring musicians and prewar record collectors. Perhaps that's because she always listed her occupation as missionary or evangelist—not musician—and devoted her time accordingly.

Dranes didn't make a record after her uncredited 1930 duet with F. W. McGee on "Fifty Miles of Elbow Room" and rarely played public concerts, drifting into an obscurity which suggests that what happens in church stays in church.

During the 1930s, Dranes was valuable to COGIC as a "planter," drawing crowds and setting an ecstatic tone at new churches. She

rizona Dranes
Blind, she learned to play at the age of 8.
Her fiery performances, often playing piano with her elbows and leaping mid song when the spirit overtook her, inspired a young Rosetta Tharpe
truth

worked closely with Bishop Riley F. Williams, who opened dozens of Pentecostal sanctuaries in Alabama, Georgia, and Ohio, like he owned the Holy Ghost franchise. For a spell in the '40s Dranes lived in Cleveland, where she once played at a massive baptism on the shores of Lake Erie, with Bishop Charles H. Mason presiding from a yacht on the lake.

Pentecostal Rhythms

There's no way to overstate how much Dranes's music was driven by her affiliation to the first black-founded Christian denomination in the US. The "saints," as the COGIC faithful call each other, become "slain in the spirit," falling out, running down the aisles, banging on tambourines, and uttering the Hebraic-sounding "glossolalia." When Sister Dranes flowed all that emotion through her piano and voice, spiritual possession had a key witness.

While the dominant Baptist and Methodist churches of the time were looking to distance themselves from the dark days of captivity and servitude, COGIC founder Charles H. Mason, the son of slaves, believed in embracing the past all the way to West Africa. Pentecostal dancing was called "shouting" because it was based on the Ring Shout of slave services.

The Pentecostal movement came out of the Azusa Street Revival in Los Angeles, which was tagged "the American Jerusalem" for the thousands of seekers who descended on the City of Angels from 1906 to 1909. COGIC founder Mason attended the around-the-clock services, led by a black, one-eyed preacher from Houston named William J. Seymour. Mason returned to his Holiness Church in Jackson, Mississippi, with a new Pentecostal message: speaking in tongues is the only true evidence of being baptized.

The doctrine is based on the story of Pentecost in the New Testament's Book of Acts. Fifty days after Passover, the eleven apostles and Christ's mother Mary gathered in Jerusalem, where the house in which they were sitting was filled with a strong wind from heaven. "And then appeared unto them cloven tongues like as of fire . . ." it's written in Acts. "And they were all filled with the Holy Ghost and began to speak in other tongues, as the Spirit granted them utterance." News reports on the Azusa Street Revival described a racially mixed congregation (which in itself was a story at the time), " . . . mouthing a creed which it would seem no sane mortal could understand."

The Holiness sect believed that besides conversion to Christianity, a conscious physical experience of "sanctification" was required for entry into heaven. But when the congregation was split over Mason's third act, the speaking in tongues, he started his own sect, taking the "Church of God in Christ" name with him.

Among the Mississippi parishioners who followed Mason to Memphis was Emmet Morey (E. M.) Page, who would figure heavily in Dranes's rise as a COGIC musician. Page was COGIC's Overseer for Texas and Oklahoma when Dranes became known, and he sent her all over the state. In the mid-1920s, Dranes spent a lot of time on the Interurban train between Dallas, where she sang for Page's COGIC church in the neighborhood now known as State-Thomas, and Fort Worth, where she wrecked praise at Rev. Samuel Crouch's Trezevant Hill Church of God In Christ on West Rosedale Street.

Dranes was on the ground floor of Pentecostalism's rise, but when she died from a stroke in 1963 at age seventy-four there was no obituary that can be found, not even in church publications. Nothing in the papers about the pioneer who could claim as a legacy the rich tradition of female pianists on gospel records. While most great keyboardists of R&B and jazz were and are male, the gospel field counts Roberta Martin, Clara Ward, Evelyn Starks, and Mahalia Jackson's pianist Mildred Falls as all-time greats.

Among those whose ears perked up in August 1926 when OKeh released the first two 78s by "the Blind Race Evangelist" was Thomas A. Dorsey, who would go on to be called "the Father of Gospel" after penning such standards as "Peace in the Valley," "Precious Lord, Take My Hand," and "If You See My Savior."

In a 1961 interview, Dorsey gave Dranes some credit for opening his mind to laying secular styles under religious themes. Although he was a Baptist, Dorsey liked to step inside the heat of sanctified services for inspira-

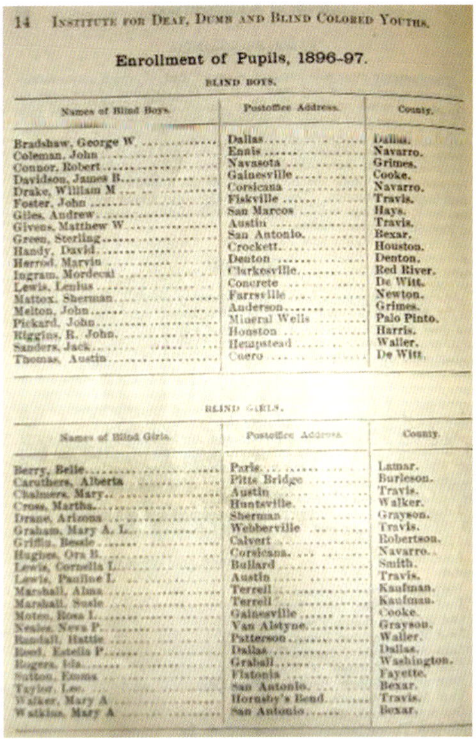
14 INSTITUTE FOR DEAF, DUMB AND BLIND COLORED YOUTHS.

Enrollment of Pupils, 1896-97.

BLIND BOYS.

Names of Blind Boys.	Postoffice Address.	County.
Bradshaw, George W	Dallas	Dallas.
Coleman, John	Ennis	Navarro.
Connor, Robert	Navasota	Grimes.
Davidson, James B.	Gainesville	Cooke.
Drake, William M	Corsicana	Navarro.
Foster, John	Fiskville	Travis.
Giles, Andrew	San Marcos	Hays.
Givens, Matthew W	Austin	Travis.
Green, Sterling	San Antonio.	Bexar.
Handy, David	Crockett	Houston.
Herrod, Marvin	Denton	Denton.
Ingram, Mordecai	Clarkesville	Red River.
Lewis, Lenius	Concrete	De Witt.
Mattox, Sherman	Farrsville	Newton.
Melton, John	Anderson	Grimes.
Pickard, John	Mineral Wells	Palo Pinto.
Riggins, R. John	Houston	Harris.
Sanders, Jack	Hempstead	Waller.
Thomas, Austin	Cuero	De Witt.

BLIND GIRLS.

Names of Blind Girls.	Postoffice Address.	County.
Berry, Belle	Paris	Lamar.
Caruthers, Alberta	Pitts Bridge	Burleson.
Chalmers, Mary	Austin	Travis.
Cross, Martha	Huntsville	Walker.
Drane, Arizona	Sherman	Grayson.
Graham, Mary A. L.	Webberville	Travis.
Griffin, Bessie	Calvert	Robertson.
Hughes, Ora B.	Corsicana	Navarro.
Lewis, Cornelia L.	Bullard	Smith.
Lewis, Pauline L	Austin	Travis.
Marshall, Alma	Terrell	Kaufman.
Marshall, Susie	Terrell	Kaufman.
Moten, Rosa L.	Gainesville	Cooke.
Neales, Neva P.	Van Alstyne	Grayson.
Randall, Hattie	Patterson	Waller.
Reed, Estella P.	Dallas	Dallas.
Rogers, Ida	Graball	Washington.
Sutton, Emma	Flatonia	Fayette.
Taylor, Lee	San Antonio.	Bexar.
Walker, Mary A	Hornsby's Bend	Travis.
Watkins, Mary A	San Antonio	Bexar.

tion, as did his protégé Mahalia Jackson. "If I can put some of what she does and mix it with the blues," Dorsey said, recalling his first exposure to Dranes, "I'll be able to come up with a gospel style."

Dorsey's genius was that his songwriting and arrangements were so sophisticated that churchgoers didn't initially realize his music was based in blues, "the devil's music." During the Depression, folks didn't want to hear reality, they wanted to escape it, and Dorsey gave sacred music a touch of Gershwin and Berlin.

Meanwhile, Dranes's style of raw, sanctified music was sent back from the studio to the Holiness/Pentecostal churches that popped up all over urban neighborhoods after World War I. In an interview with Gayle Wald for the Rosetta Tharpe biography *Shout, Sister, Shout*, churchgoer Camille Roberts recalled a Dranes performance at Roberts Temple in the 1930s. "Along comes a woman, I can't remember her name, but she was blind and she was from Texas, and she could just make the piano talk," Wald quoted Roberts. "She'd get so good she'd just hit it with her elbows."

Although their playing was as different as fire and glass, Dranes and Dorsey together formed the foundation of gospel piano accompaniment, according to a 2009 doctorate dissertation by Idella Johnson with the weighty title "Development of African American Gospel Piano Style (1926–1960): A Socio-Musical Analysis of Arizona Dranes and Thomas Dorsey."

A church music director and pianist herself, Johnson wrote that the gospel piano style "acquired its motivic and rhythmic impetus from Dranes and its blues quality and coloring from Dorsey."

The Goods Before the God

Dranes and her piano told a story, HIS story. But her own biography has been a gap-filled guessing game, for the most part. Much has been written and analyzed about how Dorsey's background from preacher's son to in-demand blues player informed his gospel direction after spiritual rebirth. But there has been very little information about how Dranes brought the barrelhouse to the altar. She's been sketched as a creation of sanctified storefronts, learning to pound away the demons on a tattered upright, while the sounds of sin seeped through the wall from the juke joint next door.

In most previously published accounts, Dranes was a raw twenty or twenty-one-year-old when she first stepped inside a Chicago recording studio. That her middle name was "Juanita" was all the evidence some needed to report she was half Mexican.

This information traveled from the first Dranes reissue, *Barrel House Piano With Sanctified Singing* on Herwin in 1976, to Document's *Complete Recorded Works* set in 1993.

The truth is that Dranes was classically trained, in both voice and piano, from ages seven to twenty-three, which explains why her singing was so impeccably punctuated, her playing so fluid and instinctive.

After graduating from the Institute for Blind Colored Youths in Austin in 1910, Dranes returned to her hometown of Sherman, near the Oklahoma border, and no doubt plied her most marketable trade. She certainly didn't learn to play ragtime, barrelhouse, and stride piano at the blind school.

No young primitive spitfire, Dranes was thirty-seven years old when she made those

HEAR AND ENJOY MUSICAL CONCERT

—FEATURING—

Arizona Dranes, Blind Pianist and Radio Star, of Cleveland, Ohio At City Auditorium, March 29, 8 P.M.

Miss Dranes Is a Regular Feature of Station WHK, of Cleveland, WAGA of Atlanta, and WGN, Birmingham. TO HEAR HER IS TO GET THE THRILL OF YOUR LIFE.

Little Albert Jewel, 14-Year-Old Soloist, of Atlanta, Will Be a Special Feature!

THIS CONCERT IS UNDER THE SPONSORSHIP OF REV. J. H. DELL, CHURCH OF GOD IN CHRIST, FOR THE BENEFIT OF THE CHURCH.

GENERAL ADMISSION 30c (Plus Tax)

Special Reservation for White People

Don't Miss This Grand Musical Concert

first landmark recordings. Evidence, as best we can expect this many years later, shows she was a relatively recent convert to Pentecostalism when she first recorded in 1926. Man had created the skilled musician before the Holy Ghost made her play with such fire.

"A School and Not an Asylum"

Arizona Dranes was the youngest of three children born to Milton and Cora Drane, who divorced when Arizona was young. Milton Jr. was the oldest, followed a year later by Millie. Father Milton Drain, as his surname was spelled (even on his death certificate after he was hit by a train in 1935), remarried and lived in Sherman, a block away from his first family. Arizona added the "s" to her surname after she left school.

Considering her tough landing in life, being born blind could've been a blessing for "Arazoni," as she was called (even on enrollment records in 1910). She certainly received the best free education a black person in Texas could at the time. Founded and funded by the Texas legislature in 1887, the blind institute was "a school and not an asylum" (though the students were sometimes termed "inmates").

The age range to attend the school, on 108 acres four miles north of the state capitol, was seven to twenty one, but Dranes, whose birth year changed from 1889 (1900 Census) to 1891 (1910 Census), stayed until she was twenty-three, perhaps fudging her birth year to delay the dire conditions that awaited in Sherman or Greenville, Texas, where her family lived for a few years. Because she needed to at least look seven years old in 1896, we know Dranes's death certificate, putting her birth year at 1894, was wrong.

Her schooling at the institute focused heavily on music, which was seen as a way, along with various handicrafts, that a blind person could make a living. Dranes was studying octaves and vocal tone production as an eight-year-old. By age ten she was tinkering with sonatas by Mozart, Beethoven, and Chopin, as well as modern compositions by Liszt and Rubinstein. To build her voice and breath control, she was taught the Italian vocal method and was singing arias by her third year at the school, according to curriculum records kept at the Texas State Library in Austin.

It's unlikely her parents, both born into slavery, were aware that such a school, 260 miles to the south, was available to their sightless daughter. Arizona was almost certainly sponsored by Sherman teacher J. W. McKinney, who taught at the Frederick Douglass School, where Dranes would've attended if she wasn't blind. McKinney, who was also the head of the black Mason Lodge of Texas, spoke at the blind school's 1902 commencement (when Dranes was eleven or thirteen), urging students to make full use of whatever gifts God had given. He ended his speech with a downplay of the era's racism.

"The fact that you are here, my friends, surrounded by all the comforts and facilities at public expense, these spacious buildings and beautiful grounds furnished for you, gives lie to (the belief that) whites have no regard for the rights of blacks," he said.

Bishop Mason sent E. M. Page to Dallas two years after Dranes graduated. The efforts to spread the Pentecostal message of spirit possession by Page's predecessor had been met with derision and even a tent-torching. Pentecostal "holy rollers" were becoming a "savage" embarrassment to mainline black churchgoers. But Page, a progressive thinker who stressed social uplift through education and community involvement, gained respect in Dallas's black Christian community. When he arrived in Texas in January 1914, there were only about eight missions in the state and not a single proper church. By 1919, there were thirty-five COGIC churches in Texas.

Page would become a key figure in Dranes's rise as a COGIC songleader, but that wouldn't be for several years after he arrived. He first started hearing about this dynamic performer in 1923, when Dranes followed Pastor J. Austin Love down from Wichita Falls to Fort Worth. What a godsend Dranes must've been for preachers who could reinforce their sermons by introducing the musical embodiment of what they'd been talking about. Her mix of technique and hysteria got the spirit to manifest itself in a hurry.

"Jesus knew what I needed most/Filled my soul with the Holy Ghost"

It was 1922 in Wichita Falls, "the City Built on Faith," when Arizona Dranes went to live with a woman, most likely a cousin, named Elve Doran. (Arizona's parents couldn't read or write, so when the family name was written down it was as it sounded. In the black southern dialect of the time, Doran would be pronounced "Drane.") The pair remained roommates for years, moving together to Chicago in 1930.

Wichita Falls had a growing COGIC presence thanks to charismatic preacher Love, who started with four believers in a living room in 1918, but had a packed First Church of God in Christ at 413 Humphries Street by the time Dranes arrived. This was almost certainly the church where the first Pentecostal music star was converted.

Researching personal history on an obscure, black, 1920s gospel musician is an often fruitless task. You never find that box of photos and letters you daydream about on long drives to small towns, but get what you can

May 4, 1926.

Arizona Dranes,
℅ Rev. Samuel Crouch,
P. O. Box 1041,
Fort Worth, Texas.

Dear Miss Dranes:-

We have heard of you as a pianist and your excellent rendition of spiritual songs in connection with your church.

Likewise, we are particularly interested at this time in the recording of spiritual songs of your church for phonograph records under the trademark "Okeh". We have a recording laboratory here in Chicago and thought it possible that you might be interested to the extent of coming to see us and possibly recording the sacred numbers which you are accustomed to and in this way you might assist in promoting and extending the work of your church to a very much greater degree. Likewise, through our affiliations and our interest in particular classes of records you possibly would consent to attend services at our local churches thereby affording the church members of the race of this city an opportunity to hear your extraordinary and wonderful playing and portrayal of the gospel numbers or songs of the church inasmuch as your playing is so distinctive.

We would like very much to hear from you as to whether or not you would entertain the idea or the possibility of your coming to Chicago in connection with recording of phonograph records and also playing at the services of our church or churches here. Can we hear from you at your earliest convenience on this subject.

Kindly address your reply to the writer and forward same in the enclosed stamped envelope.

Very truly yours,

CONSOLIDATED TALKING MACHINE CO.

EAF-HL

from census records and city directories and common sense. And sometimes you get lucky.

The 1921 Sherman city directory shows Arizona Dranes living at 534 Brockett Street and working as an actress. An actress? That info proves that Dranes was not yet a member of the Pentecostal church at age thirty-two, said COGIC historian Glenda Goodson of Dallas.

"The church would have never allowed that," said Goodson. "We couldn't even go to theaters." Being a saint meant completely rejecting popular culture, even the radio. Wearing boxlike white or black dresses, with white cotton stockings, Pentecostal women followed the motto, "Christ all in all; no more I, but Christ."

Could it have been a misprint in the directory? Actress seems an odd job for a blind black woman in a midsized Texas town circa 1921. But a piece to the puzzle could be found in an October 1920 community theater column in Billboard magazine. It reports that a new theater troupe, the Sherman Players, took over the Liberty Airdome theater on East Pecan Street, five blocks from where Dranes lived. Well-rounded by her schooling and freelance piano work, Dranes probably played ragtime, blues, and barrelhouse during downtimes at the theater and maybe also got on stage as the token black female character. Actress was a more respectable occupation to report to the city directory than musician.

Within two years, however, Dranes was a fulltime singing missionary. The Wichita Falls directory of 1923 shows no trace of Dranes, Doran, or Reverend Love, because they were down in Fort Worth, where Elder Page had sent Love to oversee construction of the White Street Holiness Church. (Although there's one main difference in doctrines—the speaking of tongues—Pentecostal and Holiness are often used interchangeably. The White Street Church is now called Greater Love Church of God in Christ.)

That must've been some grand church reopening with Dranes displaying the saucy new language of gospel music. Just as a preacher has stock phrases that he'll interject into otherwise improvised sermons, Dranes had an array of musical tricks she'd throw in to get the congregations going, including her favorite 1-6-5-1 octave bass line for propulsion. Since most sanctified churches could afford only one instrument, the piano was its orchestra. Under Dranes's playing hands the black and white keys became a symphony of harmony, rhythm, melody, and tone, but mostly rhythm. Her left-hand ostinato—contantly repeating a melodic fragment—was hypnotic.

She also picked up a middle name during those early years, perhaps in homage to White Street Church mother Juanita Harris. COGIC church leaders usually went with two initials and a surname, and Dranes was born without a middle name.

Sharing a Pentecostal Protégé with the World

In a September 1926 article in the *Fort Worth Star-Telegram*, George H. Bradford of OKeh Records' parent Consolidated Talking Machine Company said he was home in Chicago listening to the radio on New Year's Eve 1925 when WBAP broadcast a COGIC meeting from Samuel Crouch's church, featuring Arizona Dranes. "The blending of religious airs with syncopation . . . was startling," the paper reported. "Bradford said he had never heard music quite like this." The exec alerted OKeh's race records supervisor Richard M. Jones (who wrote blues classic "Trouble In Mind"), who worked with Crouch, to get Dranes up to Chicago to record.

Page sent the label a letter of endorsement which read: "Since she is Deprived Of Her Natural Sight, the Lord Has Given Her A Spiritual Sight that all Churches Enjoy. She is Loyal and Obedient, Our Prayers Ascend for her."

Although it's been reported that Jones heard Dranes in Fort Worth on a talent scout tour, the first time he'd ever heard her perform was when he produced her in the studio on June 17, 1926. Jones had his hands full up in Chicago that year preparing a group he'd organized called Louis Armstrong and His Hot Five.

The first band under Armstrong's name, and featuring the great Kid Ory on trombone, the Hot Five recorded three tracks in the same studio, with the same producer, the day before Dranes made her recording debut.

Two days in one room in Chicago and neither jazz nor gospel would ever be the same again. Rock and roll pianist and historian Rev. Billy C. Wirtz called the Dranes sessions "the first-known recorded examples of piano figures, rhythms, and melodies adopted by everyone from Jerry Lee Lewis to Mahalia Jackson and Hank Williams."

Dranes was constantly on the road in the mid-1920s, playing in churches all over Texas, Arkansas, Oklahoma, Alabama, and Tennessee. When advising her of plans to record a second Chicago session in November 1926, Bradford ended by saying, "I am sending a copy of this letter to the three different addresses that you gave us so as to be sure to reach you."

Dranes was in Dallas when OKeh contacted her a month after her first session to tell her some good news. "My dear Miss Dranes," Bradford wrote. "The samples of your records just came in today and they are truly wonderful."

The correspondence between artist and label, which writer Malcolm Shaw obtained access to for a 1970 article in *Storyville* magazine, wasn't always so warm and encouraging. Dranes had to almost beg for money sometimes and detailed various ailments that kept her from playing. On September 6, 1926, a month after her first two 78s ("John Said He Saw a Number"/ "My Soul Is a Witness For the Lord" and "It's All Right Now"/ "Sweet Heaven Is My Home") were released to promising sales, Dranes sent a letter to Bradford asking for a $50 advance. "This is very necessary and I hope you can do this for me," she wrote. Bradford declined, writing that an advance "is against one of our most strict rules and policies."

In November 1926, Columbia Records bought OKeh (named after the initials of founder Otto K. E. Heinemann and pronounced "okay") in part because of its pioneering black music department. OKeh remained independent for several years, but then came personnel changes that immediately affected Dranes's recording output. Her producer Richard Jones was out as recording director, replaced by Tommy Rockwell, who would soon start managing Satchmo.

In Sickness and Debt

In February 1928, a frustrated Dranes, who was owed money, wrote to Bradford: "Of coarse I didn't know anything about record making or prices on them and I didn't even consult our white friends down here," she typed (or dictated) from Memphis. "I took what you said about everything and was confidence that you would treat me fair. Now I'm asking that you please consider me as I am disable to work and have to be confined to my room."

But Bradford was no longer with the label. Elmer Fearn, who owned Consolidated Talking Machine Company, replied that he would send Rockwell, who was in Memphis recording Mississippi John Hurt, with the money she was owed. Rockwell visited Dranes, but she was still broke after he left. "He offered to let me have money, providing I record," Dranes wrote back, "but I am not able to record."

Fearn immediately sent Dranes $60. Her records had sold well, and he wanted her back in the studio when she felt up to it.

As COGIC overseer for Oklahoma, as well as Texas, Page sent Dranes in 1928 to Oklahoma City, where she lived on East Second Street, the R&B/ jazz haven known as "Deep Deuce." She may have heard a young guitar player on the street named Charlie Christian, who also came from Texas, or blues shouter Jimmy Rushing.

More likely, they heard her. In a 2003 interview, Helen Davis, then ninety, recalled seeing A. J . Dranes at Page's church in Oklahoma City in the 1920s. "She'd get the whole place shouting," Davis recalled. "She was a blind lady, see, and she'd let the spirit overtake her. She'd jump up from that piano bench when it hit her." Such displays masked the formal musical training that gave Dranes such command.

Dranes recorded sixteen tracks in just three sessions—June 17 and November 15, 1926, and July 3, 1928—for OKeh. Each time in the studio, she used a different backing configuration, but the piano and her voice were always dominant.

Dranes recorded two solo piano instrumentals on the first session, including "Crucifixion," which would become her signature song through inclusion on various compilations in recent years. On four tracks that June day she was loosely backed by producer Jones and noted blues singer Sara Martin, who had a 1922 hit with Fats Waller's "T'ain't Nobody's Bizness If I Do."

When OKeh sent her back to Chicago for round two, Dranes brought along F. W. McGee, a COGIC minister she probably met in Oklahoma. Dranes, McGee, and the Jubilee Singers recorded four tunes in the quintessential call and response vein used in Pentecostal congregational singing. "Lamb's Blood Has Washed Me Clean," in which Dranes declares "Jesus Christ knew what I needed most/ Filled my soul with the Holy Ghost," is awash in a spiritual ecstasy that would be considered almost barbaric for the times.

Raised in Hillsboro, Texas, Ford Washington McGee was a Methodist minister on his 1917 draft registration card, but by the 1920 census he was preaching for the Pentecostal side in Cleveland County, Oklahoma.

McGee was living in Chicago in 1926, preaching from revival tents and building a following which included Katie Bell Nubin. By the time Dranes moved to Chicago in 1929, McGee had built a COGIC temple on Vincennes Avenue on the South Side. Dranes's South Street-Lawrence Avenue apartment was just blocks away, so she surely played there, in addition to Roberts Temple.

Dranes helped McGee get a deal with OKeh and played on the singing preacher's first single "Lion of the Tribe of Judah" in 1927. But McGee soon moved to the Victor label, becoming one of the country's most famous preachers. His 1929 recording of "Jonah In the Belly of the Whale" sold over 100,000 copies.

Dranes's third and last session—credited to "Arizona Dranes and Choir," though it was really just Dranes, a splendid, unidentified mandolinist and a few female voices—showed that she was developing as an artist beyond a Pentecostal pounder. Such cuts as "Just Look" and "I Shall Wear a Crown" are fuller, more melodic than her earlier stomps.

The standout track is "He Is My Story," a rewriting of "Blessed Assurance" by blind hymn writer Fanny Crosby. Where the Crosby version has a chorus of "This is my story/ This is my song," Dranes makes it all about God. "He is my story/ He is my song," she sang with a voice quivering like an arrow at impact.

Par for Dranes's career, OKeh didn't release "Story," her most commercially viable track.

Sanctified Blues was a Dallas Thing

The relationship between OKeh and Dranes didn't end particularly well. A month after the final session, a backing musician went to Fearn's office and asked to be paid what he was owed. Fearn had given Dranes money to pay the session singers and mandolin player.

"The money u gave for them, they got every dime of it," an upset Dranes wrote Fearn from Oklahoma City, then added, "I promised to give them some of my money because they seem not to be satisfied with what they got." Dranes added that the women on the session were without complaint. "I didn't want you to think I would do any crooked work or tell a false about anything. I will be in Chicago on the 20th if nothing happens to me."

Based on style, Coley Jones of the Dallas String Band is the most widely speculated guest on mandolin. Dranes was almost certainly aware of Jones's playing. Before she was signed to her recording contract ($25 per released side), Dranes's address was next door to Page's church at the corner of Thomas and Ellis Avenues in the Freedmantown section of Dallas. The bordering district to the south was the blues hotbed of Deep Ellum, where Coley Jones, Blind Lemon Jefferson, Leadbelly, Bessie Tucker, Little Hat Jones, Hattie Burleson, Lillian Glinn, and other blues greats played on street corners and in juke joints.

As one guided by her ears, she certainly took in the blues, stride, ragtime, and barrelhouse coming from doorways when she joined her church on soul-saving missions in the red light district.

The cross-pollination of gospel and blues is exemplified by a remark by electric blues guitar pioneer T-Bone Walker that the first time he heard boogie-woogie piano was at a Pentecostal church in Dallas. He either heard Arizona Dranes or someone she influenced.

Her recordings attest that she was also fond

of another form of music with roots in Texas: ragtime. Although Scott Joplin (1867–1917) of Texarkana didn't invent the genre, which was based on an Afro-Euro mixture of jigs slaves danced to and Sousa marches, Joplin's emphasis on syncopation and cross rhythms refined it as a piano form. The left hand recalled the stomp of dancers, while the right hand played fiddle parts.

The first African American musical style to be considered popular music, ragtime made a splash at the 1893 Columbian Expo in Chicago and quickly pulled itself out of the brothels and riverboats and into the mainstream. Joplin's 1899 composition "Maple Leaf Rag" sold more than a million copies of sheet music and created a national sensation that was still going strong in the 1920s.

Black Baptist and Methodist churches of the time wouldn't think of including ragtime (AKA "whorehouse piano") at their services. But early Pentecostals erased the divide between secular and sacred because, in their perspective, all experience was religious. They could only dance at church, so they snatched the good stuff from the devil, colored in deep devotion, and had a Holy Ghost Party every Sunday and Wednesday. The "tongue people" started a musical renaissance that gave birth to soul music and rock and roll.

Congregational Compositions

At Azusa Street in 1907, Mason was one of the only converts whose church was legally incorporated, so he ended up ordaining more than three hundred white ministers into his denomination. In its first seven years, COGIC services were racially integrated, with whites usually sitting in the balcony because of segregation laws.

When the US joined World War I in 1917, the word got out to the FBI that Bishop Mason had a lawyer from Germany and was preaching against US involvement in the war. Claiming that Mason predicted a US defeat as payback for how it treated blacks, the FBI arrested Mason on a Sedition Act violation.

But they couldn't prove anything, and the charges were dropped. Mason had endured this kind of harassment for years because of his integrated parish, so he was a little relieved when the white members started leaving to form the Assemblies of God. Giving his blessing, the Bishop spoke at their first conference in Hot Springs, Arkansas, in 1914.

By 1920, COGIC was entirely black and dedicated twenty days every year to a big Azusa-like gathering. The National Convocation is held in Memphis every year, from November 25 until December 14. It's a harvest festival of sorts, just like Pentecost in Christ's time.

The convocations are where songleaders from all over the country share songs they have written or learned. Until fairly recently, COGIC congregations didn't use hymn books, so this is how Dranes found most of her material, which she would then adapt to her style and sentiment. The history of gospel music is a history of reinterpretation, as there are dozens of different versions of the same songs floating around without true ownership. Dranes is listed on the Consolidated Music Publishing contracts as the writer of the songs she recorded, but aside from the ones she was known to make up in the heat of services, most of the material really belonged to the COGIC congregations.

Pentecostals have to make their own fun, so a highlight of the convocation was always the nightly musical performances. From midnight until the sun came up, such performers as Dranes, electric guitarist Elder Utah Smith, singers Madame Ernestine Washington and Goldia Haynes, plus the piano shout duo of Elders Curry and Beck would keep the praise songs going strong.

Perusing the annual convocation yearbooks kept at the McGlothen Temple Library, one can see Dranes's prominence diminish greatly through the years. Even though she was closely associated with three of the five original COGIC Bishops—E. M. Page, R. F. Williams, and W. M. Roberts of Chicago—there's no mention of her in any of the church histories, even those focusing on women in COGIC.

Partly that's because she was never a member of the almighty COGIC Women's Department, where names like Mother Lizzie Woods Robinson and Mother Lillian Brooks Coffey are almost as mythical as Bishop Mason. Another carryover from slave tradition, COGIC gave women great responsibility, but reserved ultimate authority for a male leader. Women didn't "preach," they would "teach," from a secondary lectern, never the pulpit.

"Sweet Heaven Is My Home"

There were Dranes sightings here and there as the years wore on, but, really, if you weren't a member of a black Pentecostal church in Texas, Oklahoma, Chicago, Cleveland, Memphis, Little Rock, St. Louis, Atlanta, Birmingham, or Los Angeles, you had almost no chance of ever seeing Arizona Dranes perform.

Although she played behind Madame Ernestine Washington at a Chicago COGIC women's convention in 1953, Arizona's last known public appearance was in Cleveland in 1947. She was billed as the "Famous Blind Piano Player from Chicago."

She spent the last years of her life in Los Angeles, where her old friend Bishop Crouch bought the Lincoln Theater on South Central Avenue in 1961 and turned it into the Crouch Temple.

Dranes was not mentioned again in the convocation yearbook after 1953. Her death certificate noted that she'd suffered from cerebral arteriosclerosis for years, which could've caused dementia. She was living in an assisted living facility in Signal Hill, California, when she had the stroke that killed her on July 27, 1963. She had never married, and her occupation at the time of death was "missionary."

Arizona Dranes was buried at the Paradise Memorial Park in Santa Fe Springs, California, but no one knows exactly where her body is today.

Investigators discovered in 1995 that the cemetery had reached capacity ten years earlier, so the owners were digging up bodies in the older sections and reselling plots.

According to the 1963 burial record, Dranes was laid to rest in section 183, block 4 and lot F-3. According to Warren Clark, a researcher for Find a Grave Inc., that was one of the recycled plots. Dranes's remains were most likely moved to a mass grave.

Ghastly to think such a pious force of nature would meet such a cruel state of disregard, but Pentecostals, like all Christians, see the body as just a bag for the soul.

She was the Holy Ghost's favorite singer, an otherworldly vessel fueled by faith. This ragged virtuoso of touch and tone had spent her whole life getting ready for when the time came, whether it was a career as a church-wrecker or a chance to sing for God in heaven.

So that's how it ended, happily for Arizona Dranes if her beliefs were true. And here's how it started: a poor, scared, little blind girl from North Texas sat at a piano in Austin in 1896 and knew she'd never be lonely again.

CHAPTER 5

Blind Willie Johnson

Revelations in the Dark

When Jack White of the White Stripes announced at Stubb's Austin in June 2003, "It's good to be in Texas, the home of Blind Willie Johnson," you can be sure that few on hand had ever heard of the gospel blues singer/guitarist who pioneered a ferocity that still lives in modern rock.

The first songs Blind Willie recorded, on a single December day in Dallas in 1927, are more familiar because of who covered them. "Nobody's Fault But Mine" was resurrected by Led Zeppelin; Eric Clapton did "Motherless Children"; Bob Dylan turned Johnson's "Jesus Make Up My Dying Bed" into "In My Time of Dying" on his 1962 debut LP; and "If I Had My Way I'd Tear the Building Down" has been appropriated by everyone from the Grateful Dead to the Staple Singers.

Johnson's haunting masterpiece "Dark Was the Night (Cold Was the Ground)," also recorded in the first session, was chosen by musicologist Alan Lomax for an album placed aboard the *Voyager 1* in 1977 on its journey to the ends of the universe. Should extraterrestrials listen to that eerie, moaning, steel-sliding memorial to the Crucifixion, they will know almost as much about Blind Willie Johnson as we do.

Beyond five recording dates from 1927 to 1930 that yielded thirty tracks—ten each in Dallas, New Orleans, and Atlanta—the rough-voiced singer has remained something of a biographical question mark. Just finding his death certificate corrected such misinformation as his dates of birth (1897, not 1902) and death (1945, not 1949).

But finding witnesses who knew Johnson was about as easy as interviewing folks who lived through World War I. Most were dead or too old to remember. Or, like Sam Faye Kelly, the only child of Blind Willie that we know of, they were too young to realize what was going on six, seven decades ago. "I remember him singing here in the kitchen and reciting from

the Bible," said Kelly, who was seventy-two when I interviewed her in 2003. Kelly, whose mother Willie B. Harris sang backup on Blind Willie's later records, was back in Marlin, living in the falling-down house at 817 Hunter Street where she was most likely conceived. She passed away in 2005, without ever receiving a penny for her father's songs and arrangements on the albums that have sold many million copies. It's almost as if her father didn't exist.

Folks have been looking for Blind Willie Johnson since his "John the Revelator" jumped out of Harry Smith's monumental *Anthology of American Folk Music* in 1952 like a Pentecostal preacher. "Well, who's that writin'?" Blind Willie called out in a fog-cutter bass, with his amen queen Willie B. Harris responding, "John the Revelator." The repetition of those dissimilar, tent revival voices created a rhythm of dignified hardship, a struggle redeemed by faith. Thumb-picked guitar lines danced around the rough/smooth tension as the devil slid into the back pew.

This 1930 gospel recording about the Apostle who wrote the *Book of Revelation* was as lowdown dirty and hoppin' as any blues or hillbilly number on Smith's six-disc collection. Blind Willie didn't even have to play any bottleneck guitar, which would become his signature after later reissues.

Johnson's initial popularity on Columbia's 14000-D "race records" series was such that he was one of the only gospel blues artists whose '78s were reissued during the Depression (four records in 1935). He recorded eighteen months before the debut of the more celebrated Delta blues icon Charley Patton and perfected a slide guitar style with open D tuning that influenced everyone from Robert Johnson and Elmore James to Jimmy Page and Johnny Winter. Vocally, you can be sure Pat-

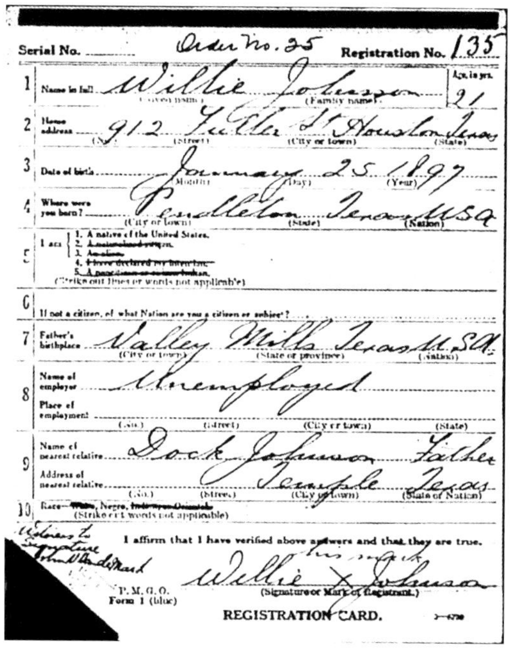
Serial No. ______ Order No. 25 Registration No. 135

1 Name in full Willie Johnson (Given name) (Family name) Age, in yrs. 21

2 Home address 912 Fuller St Houston Texas (No.) (Street) (City or town) (State)

3 Date of birth January 25 1897 (Month) (Day) (Year)

4 Where were you born? Pendleton Texas USA (City or town) (State) (Nation)

5 I am 1. A native of the United States. 2. ~~A naturalized citizen.~~ 3. ~~An alien.~~ 4. ~~I have declared my intention.~~ 5. ~~A noncitizen or citizen Indian.~~ (Strike out lines or words not applicable)

6 If not a citizen, of what Nation are you a citizen or subject? ______

7 Father's birthplace Valley Mills Texas U.S.A. (City or town) (State or province) (Nation)

8 Name of employer Unemployed
Place of employment ______ (No.) (Street) (City or town) (State)

9 Name of nearest relative Dock Johnson Father
Address of nearest relative Temple Texas (No.) (Street) (City or town) (State or Nation)

10 Race—~~White~~, Negro, ~~Indian, Oriental~~ (Strike out words not applicable)

I affirm that I have verified above answers and that they are true.

his mark
Willie X Johnson
(Signature or Mark of Registrant.)

P. M. G. O. Form 1 (blue)

REGISTRATION CARD.

ton understudy Chester Burnett took notice of Johnson's wolf-like howl.

In just three years, Blind Willie Johnson produced a significant body of work that transports the listener from ancient Africa to modern times. And yet by the release of Harry Smith's gateway drug, he was known as "the other Blind Willie" (not McTell).

Just as the *Book of Revelation* was written on a scroll fastened by seven seals, Blind Willie's story was one that begged to be unlocked. The first to try was twenty-four-year-old Samuel Charters (1929-2015), who set out for Texas in 1953 to see what he could find about two bluesmen named Johnson, who made their first records there. But while the icy trail of Robert Johnson, who recorded in San Antonio in 1936 and Dallas the next year, made even hellhounds call it a day, Charters got lucky with the gospel Johnson. Sam and his wife Ann followed leads from Dallas to Beaumont, where they eventually met Blind Willie's widow, Angeline Johnson.

The Charters-produced 1957 album *Blind Willie Johnson: His Story* (Folkways) reissued more of Johnson's music, including "If I Had My Way, I'd Tear the Building Down," which the Grateful Dead called "Samson and Delilah" when they recorded it on 1977's *Terrapin Station*. Side one concentrated on Johnson's biography, with spoken remembrances from people who knew Blind Willie, most prominently Angeline.

Rather than detail what was wrong in some of those eyewitness reports, let's tell you what we now know to be certain about Blind Willie Johnson, who died in Beaumont at age forty-eight on September 18, 1945. The truth starts with a 1918 WWI draft registration card that popped up on ancestry.com around 2007. The card's twenty-one-year-old Willie Johnson lived in Houston's Fourth Ward, a block from the red light district nicknamed "The Reservation," which seemed strange for a gospel musician. But recent findings conclude that this Willie Johnson, blind, was, indeed, Blind Willie Johnson.

We know draft card Willie is our guy because the 1935 Temple city directory lists a "Willie Johnson, musician" living at the same 308 South Fifth Street address as four other children of the man he said was his father in 1918. When Willie Johnson and Willie B. Harris had daughter Sam Faye in 1931, he said he was from Temple.

His death certificate incorrectly lists his Texas birthplace as the town of Independence, near Brenham, where Angeline was from. Blind Willie's parents were Dock Johnson and Mary King, married May 2, 1894, in Meridian, Texas, the town closest to the ranch where famed folklorist John A. Lomax grew up. The Johnsons moved about fifty miles south, to Bell County, before Willie Johnson was born in January 1897 in Pendleton.

Book II: A Haunting Masterpiece

Blind Willie sang in three distinctive voices: the gruff false bass, the soulful natural tenor, and through his expressive slide guitar, which often finished verses for him. They were the father, the son, and the Holy Ghost of his music, with Johnson a one-man Holy Trinity on the old "lining out" hymn "Dark Was the Night." His guitar preached and his inner congregation hummed in response.

There are no words in Blind Willie's "Dark," but there are lyrics to the Baptist hymn where it originated. It's about the Garden of Gethsemane, where Jesus was arrested and tormented on the night before the crucifixion.

"Dark was the night and cold was the ground/ On which the Lord was laid/ His sweat like drops of blood ran down/In agony he prayed," wrote Thomas Haweis in 1792

It's a song about the Passion, and Blind Willie nailed it on the first take in Dallas. It's a one-of-a-kind recording that's set a mood in several films, first in Pier Paolo Pasolini's 1964 Italian classic *Gospel According to St. Matthew*. Basing his soundtrack of *Paris, Texas* on "Dark," Ry Cooder called it "the most soulful, transcendent piece in all of American music."

Johnson was not the first gospel singer to play slide guitar on record. He was beat to the studio by a year and a half by Pittsburgh preacher Edward W. Clayborn and Delta player Sam "Boll Weevil Jackson" Butler. For blues, you can go back to 1923, when Louisville's Sylvester Weaver recorded "Guitar Rag" (covered by Bob Wills and the Texas Playboys as "Steel Guitar Rag" in 1936) for OKeh. Those guys were crafty and talented, but when Blind Willie started playing slide it's like he invented the dunk. He paired gifts for improvisation and control, the melody and the rhythm, in a way that's unsurpassed.

"Anybody who's ever played the bottleneck guitar with some degree of accomplishment is quoting Blind Willie to this day," said Austin slide guitarist Steve James.

Johnson grew up one county over from Blind Lemon Jefferson, and they often played on opposite street corners in Hearne, according to Adam Booker, the blind Brenham preacher interviewed by Charters in 1955. They played in the same general genre, with religious/secular lyrics being the core difference, but Jefferson didn't play the slide. And Johnson didn't make the people dance like Blind Lemon did.

Book III: Johnson & Johnson, Gospel and Blues

Jefferson and Johnson inspired Robert Johnson, who combined their styles to lay out the blueprint for Chicago blues and its offspring in November 1936 at the Gunter Hotel in San Antonio. The Mississippi guitarist's debut session, on the 23rd, produced eight tracks for Vocalion Records, including "I Believe I'll Dust My Broom," "Sweet Home Chicago," and

"Ramblin' On My Mind." In June the next year, Johnson went to Dallas to record the rest of his canon, including "Love in Vain Blues," "Hellhound on My Trail," and "Stop Breakin' Down Blues." Blind Willie's monumental debut session ten years earlier was the butterfly wings to set the Big Bang of blues rock in motion.

Even though his playing, always on a Stella guitar, inspired a host of Delta blues men, Blind Willie sang only religious songs, which explains a big part of his relative obscurity. His raspy evangelical bark and dramatic guitar were designed to draw in milling, mulling masses on street corners, not to charm casual roots rock fans decades later.

But he had his time. When Willie Johnson was booked for the December 1928 sessions for Columbia, he had already sold an average of 15,000 copies of his first three '78s (at seventy-five cents each), and so he was treated with an earner's respect. He had a car and driver, and the label put him and Willie B. up at the Delmonico Hotel at 302 North Central Avenue in Deep Ellum.

The couple proved to be vocal soulmates on four tracks recorded on December 5, 1928, including "Jesus Is Coming Soon" (about the 1918 Spanish Flu epidemic) and "Keep Your Lamp Trimmed and Burning." The Columbia recording logs also list two tracks, unnamed and unreleased, as by Blind Texas Marlin, but we'll never know if that was Blind Willie singing some blues on the side. The notes and papers of Frank Buckley Walker disappeared, he said in the interview with Mike Seeger. A big chunk of music history gone. Columbia lost or threw away the Blind Willie Johnson masters long ago, and all his CD reissues were made by digitizing 78 RPM records loaned by collectors.

The search goes on, but what we still don't know about Blind Willie Johnson could sink the Titanic. The mystery has made him more spirit than mortal, a folk hero.

The most legendary story about Blind Willie, which Angeline told to Charters in 1955, was that he was blinded by a stepmother who "throwed lye water in Willie's face and put his eyes out." But Willie B. Harris told fan Dan Williams in the '70s that her former husband became blind from looking at the sun through a piece of glass during an eclipse. Indeed, a partial eclipse was seen over Texas in August 1905, when BWJ was eight, the year he lost his sight.

Angeline said Willie's mother had died when he was a boy and his father remarried.

Dock Johnson, indeed, took a new wife, Catherine Garrett, in June 1908. But in the 1911 Temple directory, Dock Johnson was living with a wife named Mary, before going back to Catherine two years later.

By 1915, everything seemed patched up, as Willie Johnson was listed as living with Dock and Catherine at 316 West Avenue D in Temple, just one hundred yards from the train depot. He wouldn't stay long. He was eighteen and ready to make some money on the streets of Texas with a pocket knife, a tin cup, and a beat-up old guitar.

Book IV: "Where the Cotton South Meets the Cattle West"

Temple is named after Bernard Temple, who was chief engineer of the Gulf, Colorado and Santa Fe Railway when the town was formed in 1881 out of two hundred acres of farmland the railroad had purchased. It became even more of a railroad town when the Missouri, Kansas and Texas Railway ("the Katy") laid tracks through Temple in 1882. The Atchison, Topeka and the Santa Fe had fifty-five miles of track in Bell County and went up to Fort Worth and down to Galveston, while the Katy was the main route between Dallas and San Antonio. Ragtime king Scott Joplin, from Texarkana, lived circa 1895 in Temple, where he wrote and published sheet music pieces on a commission from the MK&T. The railroads made Temple an urban hub between Waco and Austin.

The town was also in Cotton Country, on the western border of the Black Waxy Prairie. The crop was so identified with Bell County that the semipro baseball team of 1905–1907 was called the Temple Boll Weevils, after the infestation of the 1890s.

The busy season for corner singers was when the cotton came in and the streets were full of folks ready to party. Such money-making opportunities took Johnson to Hearne, Marlin, Brenham, and Navasota, as well as the big cities. Because he was blind, he rode the train at reduced fare, if he had to pay at all. "Play us that 'Titanic' song!" was probably enough to carry Blind Willie wherever he wanted to go.

Blind Willie's first marriage took him to Houston in 1917, if later census numbers are correct. According to the 1930 census, the musician said he was married at age twenty and divorced. That's approximately when the draft card said he was living in Houston, where there was plenty of work for a musician in the "anything goes" district where Johnson lived. Usually it was playing in whorehouses or medicine shows, but after the 1915 Panama Pacific Expo in San Francisco, Hawaiian steel guitar was all the rage. It's quite possible Blind Willie made money for a spell with his guitar in his lap, but his slide playing on record is more percussive, attacking, than the Island style.

Songster Mance Lipscomb (1895–1976), who enjoyed a late-life discovery by the hippie/folk crowd, recalled seeing Johnson play in front of Tex's Radio shop in Navasota, seventy miles northwest of Houston, as early as 1916. "He just had people from here to the highway. Jes' hunnuds a people standing right on the streets," Lipscomb said in his oral autobiography *I Say Me For a Parable*. "White and black. Old colored folks and young ones as well. Listenin' at his voice." Lipscomb said Johnson

walked with a stick and traveled with an older blind man. That was most likely Madkin Butler, the best gospel shouter out of Hearne.

Book V: Blind Leading the Blind

In the beginning God created the heaven and the earth. And the earth was without form and void; and darkness was upon the face of the deep. And the spirit of God moved upon the face of the waters.

—the Book of Genesis

The dominant Texas preacher of the era was John L. "Sin Killer" Griffin, who toured all over the state and possessed, according to a Houston newspaper in 1911, a voice with the power of "thunder's sullen roar." But Blind Willie had a more direct model for his pulpit-shaking bellow in the singing preacher they called Blind Butler (1873–1936). Madkin Butler showed the kid, twenty-four years his junior, how to make his voice heard above a crowd by flipping it inside out with authority. Butler was most likely the writer of "God Moves On the Water," one of Blind Willie's greatest recordings, which Waco folklorist Dorothy Scarborough published in 1919's *From a Southern Porch* folklore collection. Lipscomb recalled a night in Houston when he sang "Titanic," as he called "God Moves," with Ophelia Butler, who Mack McCormick told him was the widow of the man who wrote it.

A singer and fiddle player who was never recorded that we know of, Madkin Butler was probably the "blind singer from Hearne" who taught John A. Lomax "Boll Weevil" in 1909.

Willie B. Harris, who grew up in Franklin next to Hearne, said Blind Butler was the most highly regarded singer in Robertson County. Harris talked about the Butler/Johnson mentorship when she was interviewed in the '70s by Dallas artist and blues collector Dan Williams. "She told me they played music on the train together," Williams recalled. In 1920, Texas had 16,000 miles of railroad tracks, twice as much as any other state, and Blind Willie got around.

As many have done since, Williams trekked to Marlin to find out whatever he could about that mysterious, intense Blind Willie Johnson. "I approached a group of elderly black people near the town square, and one of them said he was related to Blind Willie's ex-wife, the one who sang on his records, and I thought I was going to meet Angeline Johnson," Williams recalled in 2003. "Nobody knew anything about a Willie B. Harris."

After hearing Harris sing along to Blind Willie's recording of "Church I'm Fully Saved Today," from their final session in Atlanta on April 20, 1930, Williams was sure Harris was the duet partner. "She talked about meeting Blind Willie McTell in Atlanta and I did some research and found out that, sure enough, McTell recorded at the same sessions," said Williams.

Charters inaccurately credited Angeline Johnson as the female background singer in his chapter on Blind Willie in 1959's seminal *The Country Blues*, but made the correction, crediting Harris, on a 1993 CD reissue for Sony Legacy. Still, it's possible that the more flamboyant Angeline was Willie's unidentified backup singer at the sessions in New Orleans in December 1929. Columbia's Walker set up a session in Dallas a week earlier, but Blind Willie chose to record in New Orleans, so he was probably living in the closer city of Beaumont as early as 1929, which is what Angeline had been saying. The New Orleans session is notable for producing the enduring "Let Your Light Shine On Me," the first song Johnson recorded in standard guitar tuning, which was a standout on the all-gospel soundtrack to the Coen Brothers' 2004 film *The Ladykiller*. The Big Easy also makes an appearance in Blind Willie lore because it's been reported—without any sourcing—that the musician was arrested for inciting a riot by singing "If I Had My Way, I'd Tear This Building Down" in front of the US Customs building in 1929.

Could Blind Willie Johnson have had an influence on Beaumont-raised trumpet player Harry James in the late '20s, early '30s? "I was brought up in Texas with the blues," the jazz legend told Merv Griffin in 1977. "Down in what they call 'Barbecue Row' I used to sit in with the guys that had the broken bottlenecks on their guitars, playing the blues; that's all we knew."

When you add up all the dates and testimony, it's very possible that Johnson was "married" to both Angeline in Beaumont and Willie B. in Marlin at the same time. There is no official record of those marriages, aside from newborn daughter Sam Faye listed as legitimate in Marlin in 1931, but couples "jumping the broom" together was a common matrimonial procedure for poor folks back then. Because of a December 2, 1932, entry in the *San Antonio Register* black newspaper, we do know Willie was married to a Mary Brown for a spell. Then, the 1937 Corpus Christi city directory has Willie Johnson, musician, living there with wife Annie (as Angeline was known by some). That makes sense because of what McCormick said in 2003: "(Blind Willie) left memories in Corpus Christi during WWII when there was a fear about Nazi submarines prowling the Gulf of Mexico. Someone must have told him submarines often listened to radio stations to triangulate their position. He went on the air with new verses to one of his songs, probably 'God Moves on the Water,' offering grace to his audience, then followed with a dire warning to the crew of any listening U-boat with 'Can't Nobody Hide from God.'"

In the 1945 Beaumont city directory Johnson is listed as a Reverend living at the House of Prayer at 1440 Forest. According to his death certificate later that year, Johnson died from malarial fever, with syphilis and blindness as contributing factors.

But Angeline Johnson painted an even bleaker picture of Willie Johnson's final days. She told Charters that her husband died from pneumonia after sleeping on wet newspapers the night after a fire. His life could've

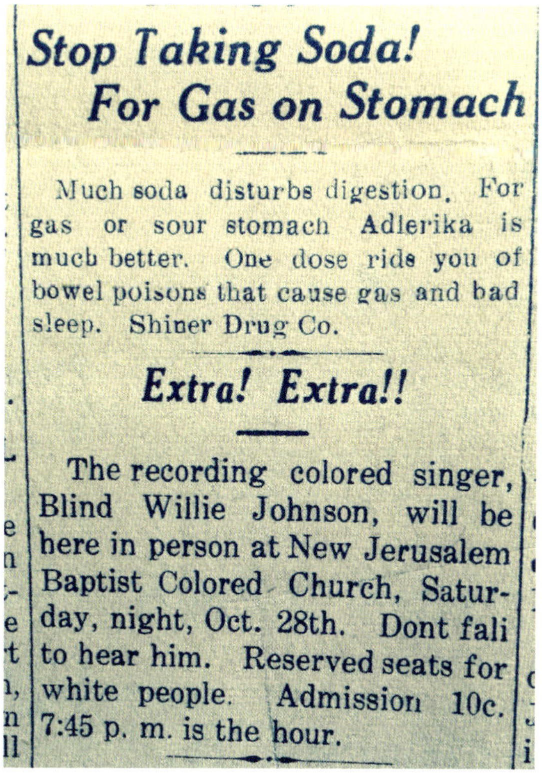

Stop Taking Soda! For Gas on Stomach

Much soda disturbs digestion. For gas or sour stomach Adlerika is much better. One dose rids you of bowel poisons that cause gas and bad sleep. Shiner Drug Co.

Extra! Extra!!

The recording colored singer, Blind Willie Johnson, will be here in person at New Jerusalem Baptist Colored Church, Saturday, night, Oct. 28th. Dont fali to hear him. Reserved seats for white people. Admission 10c. 7:45 p. m. is the hour.

been saved, she said, except he was refused service at the hospital because he was black and blind. But such a scenario was "highly unlikely," said McCormick, who had worked in a Houston emergency room in the Jim Crow era of legalized discrimination. "He would not have been turned away."

The "charred" 1440 Forest Avenue house stood until 1970, when it was torn down to make room for I-10.

The "malarial fever" cause of death seemed strange for East Texas and led many to believe Angeline Johnson's pneumonia story. But before penicillin became available to the public in the late '40s, doctors sometimes treated degenerative syphilis with injections of malaria. The high body temperatures could sometimes kill the syphilis bacteria, but the downside was that many of those treated died from malarial fever.

Book VI: Marlin and Marriages

Between his years in Temple and Beaumont, there was Marlin, perhaps the town most connected to Blind Willie this many years later. Wood Street brought the street corner gospel singer to the town thirty-seven miles northeast of Temple. With its wooden sidewalks, prostitutes hanging out of windows, and music coming out of every doorway, Wood Street of the '20s and '30s featured the most happening street scene in black Central Texas. When the Leadbelly biopic, starring Roger E. Mosley, was filmed in 1976, producers used Wood Street to portray Shreveport's infamous Fannin Street.

Marlin's a nothing town today, but during the first half of the twentieth century, after hot mineral water with reputed healing powers was discovered and bathhouses built, it became a destination for the rich, with a booming economy. The New York Giants held spring training in Marlin from 1908 to 1918 and Conrad Hilton built the nine-story Falls Hotel there in 1929. There were plenty of jobs for black folks and on Saturday night, Wood Street was hopping.

Musicians played all up and down the street, according to ninety-four-year-old James Truesdale in 2010. "He could make that guitar talk to you," the Lott native said of Blind Willie, describing a scene of people "falling out and hollerin'" to Johnson's gospel music. Two

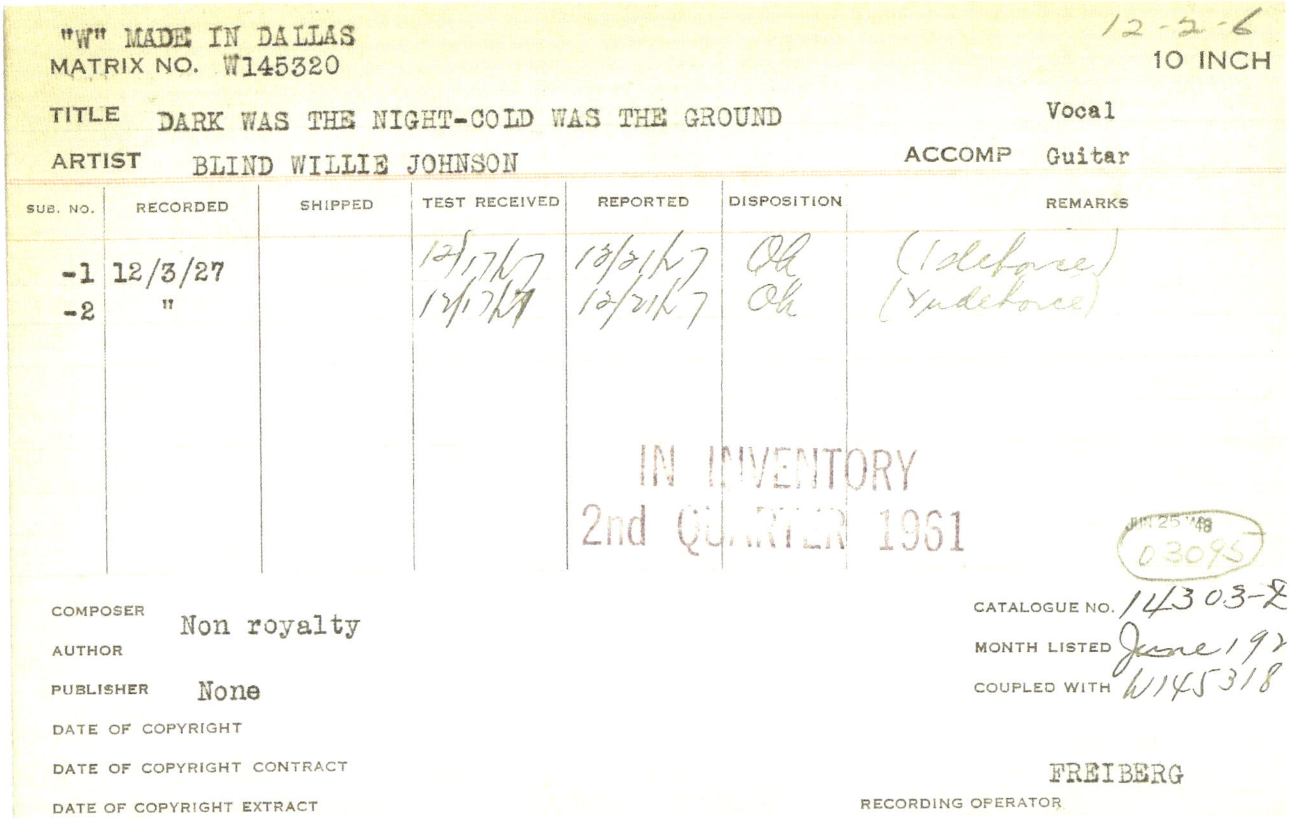

"W" MADE IN DALLAS 12-2-6

MATRIX NO. W145320 10 INCH

TITLE DARK WAS THE NIGHT-COLD WAS THE GROUND Vocal

ARTIST BLIND WILLIE JOHNSON ACCOMP Guitar

SUB. NO.	RECORDED	SHIPPED	TEST RECEIVED	REPORTED	DISPOSITION	REMARKS
-1	12/3/27		12/17/27	12/21/27	Ok	[illegible]
-2	"		12/17/27	12/21/27	Ok	[illegible]

IN INVENTORY 2nd QUARTER 1961

JUN 25 '48 03095

COMPOSER
AUTHOR Non royalty

PUBLISHER None

DATE OF COPYRIGHT

DATE OF COPYRIGHT CONTRACT

DATE OF COPYRIGHT EXTRACT

CATALOGUE NO. 14303-D

MONTH LISTED June 192

COUPLED WITH W145318

FREIBERG
RECORDING OPERATOR

blocks from the sin of Wood Street was the Falls County Baptist Association, where Truesdale said Johnson and Butler often played in a makeshift venue called the Soul Station.

When she met her future husband, Willie B. Harris worked as a bathhouse attendant and belonged to the Power House Church of God in Christ. She told Williams that she and Blind Willie began performing together at the Pentecostal church.

The last known venue of a Blind Willie Johnson concert still standing is the New Jerusalem Missionary Baptist Church in Shiner, Texas. Johnson came to Shiner from San Antonio in October 1933 to play the one hundred-capacity church for ten cents a ticket. "Reserved seating for white people," it said in the newspaper. It's conceivable Blind Willie had hundreds of shows like this after making his final recordings in April 1930. Playing music live was the only way he had to make a living, since his recordings were "non-royalty," according to Columbia session cards.

Also recently found is a clipping that describes the crowd at New York City's Hippodrome becoming "deathlike" quiet while Blind Willie Johnson sang "Nobody's Fault But Mine" circa 1938. In a 1940 interview with John A. Lomax, Blind Willie McTell said he and the other Blind Willie had been touring "from Maine to Mobile." McTell paid homage to his old friend when he cut "Motherless Children" for Atlantic in 1949. That's how long it took for word of Johnson's death to reach many of those who knew him, one reason earlier biographies had him dying in '49, not '45.

There's been only one photo found of Willie Johnson, wearing a suit and sitting at a piano with his guitar. His left pinkie appears to be straightened by a glass or steel cylinder, which is how Angeline's brother, Brenham-raised blues guitarist L. C. Robinson, said Johnson played slide. "He used to come stay with us, two, three nights, and he'd sit there and play that guitar, religious songs," Robinson told *Living Blues* in 1975 about his brother-in-law. "I was watching him with that bottle on there and started playing that way, too."

But bluesman Thomas Shaw (1908–1977) told the magazine in 1972 that Blind Willie slid a pocketknife over the strings to play slide. "Willie lived in Temple and we'd go down there to play for the country dances and school openings and all and I'd stay with him," said Shaw. "I learned that 'Just Can't Keep From Cryin' from him but I learned to pick it 'cause I didn't like the knife on it."

Listening to Johnson fretting strings and playing rhythm along with his slide, it seems unlikely he played with a knife in the studio, but it could've been a cool street-corner trick.

Book VII: The Sounds of Earth in Outer Space

Blind Willie's songs were about the love of Jesus and the hope of salvation, with a touch of Old Testament vengeance. But how many of those did he write? How many were adapted from public domain sources such as religious hymns and old "Negro spirituals"? It's certainly a question to be determined once an estate for Blind Willie Johnson is finally established.

Precedents for "Nobody's Fault But Mine," "John the Revelator," "Motherless Children," "Soul of a Man," and the topical songs "Jesus Is Coming" and "When the War Is On" haven't been found, so they can be classified as original compositions. But the majority of Johnson's twenty-nine recorded songs (he cut "You'll Need Somebody on Your Bond" twice) came from other sources. According to Max Haymes's "Roots of Blind Willie Johnson" research on earlyblues.com, the singer took three songs from the 1923 recordings of the Wiseman Sextette and covered T. E. Weems on "If I Had My Way," Arizona Dranes on "Bye and Bye, I'm Gonna See the King," and Blind Joe Taggart's "Take Your Burden To the Lord." But entertainment attorney William Krasilovsky said in 2003 that a Blind Willie estate could earn money by copyrighting his arrangements. "Does the work have distinctive fingerprints of originality that qualify for a new derivative copyright of public domain material?" he asked, reading from a copyright law book.

"Distinctive fingerprints" could be the title of a Blind Willie Johnson biography.

There was a bit of head-butting when Alan Lomax was brought aboard on the *Voyager 1* project and chucked DeBussy in favor of Peruvians and their panpipes and Chuck Berry playing rock 'n' roll. But in *Murmurs of Earth*, a book recounting the Voyager project, Carl Sagan wrote that Lomax "brought pieces so compelling and beautiful that we gave in to his suggestions more often than I would have thought possible." In the end, Lomax was responsible for fifteen of the twenty-seven musical recordings on *Voyager 1*, including the Blind Willie moaner, which Lomax said he included as the best embodiment of loneliness. Beethoven follows Blind Willie to close out *The Golden Record*.

Should aliens happen upon the *Voyager 1* and, with the record player provided, listen to "Dark Was the Night," they will know that we are a spiritual people, that we hurt and we heal, that we do indeed have souls that live long after we're buried.

This many years later, the root of Willie Johnson's blindness and his cause of death are unimportant. What he did with a guitar and a blessed bellow is all that matters. The music's so supercharged with self-expression that the truth is right there for all to hear.

CHAPTER 6

Slide Guitar From the Hawaiians to Sacred Steel

Much as the once-derided accordion became cool when the likes of Clifton Chenier and Flaco Jimenez snatched it from "The Lawrence Welk Show," the sliding steel guitar sound took off around 2002 with the "Sacred Steel" phenomenon, a new way to rock that came from a sixty-five-year-old tradition. The Campbell Brothers, Aubrey Ghent, Sonny Treadway, Calvin Cooke, Maurice "Ted" Beard and many more gospel steel players took their talents from the House of God, a black Pentecostal church with two hundred congregations in the United States, to concert stages all over the world. But the biggest star was Robert Randolph, who sported cornrows and hip-hop clothes to match a swaggering stage presence. His mother, a House of God minister, was overjoyed when a seventeen-year-old Robert started going back to church, where his rapturous pedal steel flights floored churchgoers. Not unlike Arizona Dranes, whom all Pentecostal performers followed, Randolph's chief duty was driving the congregation to heightened levels of spiritual possession. He took a few licks from Blind Willie Johnson, too, but Sacred Steel grew out of Hawaiian music, not gospel blues.

Founded in 1903 during the advent of the Pentecostal/Holiness movement and headquartered in Nashville, the House of God (originally called The Church of the Living God, the Pillar and Ground of the Truth Without Controversy) features services where churchgoers speak in tongues and do holy "shout" dances. What sets this sect apart from the other so-called "holy rollers" is the use of lap steel and pedal steel to lead the music. Psalms 150:4 says, "Praise him with stringed instruments," and the H. of G. has made a sacrament out of the strings that can weep and moan and sing. "A lot of the House of God churches couldn't

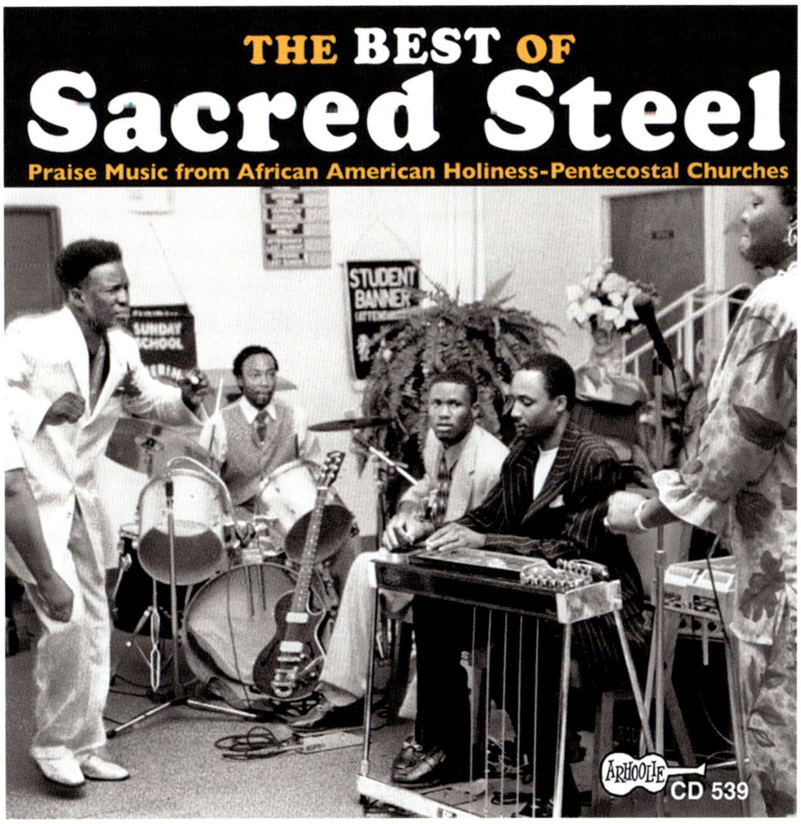

afford an organ," Randolph explained in 2002. "A steel guitar is a lot cheaper and has the same sort of sustaining sound as the organ. Plus, it sounds more like a singing voice, which is why we duet with the singers. When they slur, you slide. When they go way up, you go higher."

The lap steel was introduced to the House of God in the late '30s by Troman and Willie Eason, a pair of brothers from Philadelphia. Troman had taken lessons from a Hawaiian steel player living in Philly and showed his younger brother a few licks. Rather than follow his brother's more traditional Polynesian style, Willie played as if his music was the lyric of his soul, developing a flamboyant single string lead style that mimicked the singing voice. Willie Eason was also responsible for spreading sacred steel to the House of God hotbed of Florida (which has nearly fifty congregations). In 1940, he married Ocala, Florida, native Alyce Nelson, whose younger brother Henry Nelson became fascinated with his brother-in-law's "talking guitar" style. Nelson added a driving strum to the style of gospel steel that would become a House of God trademark, passed down through the generations.

Soon after human beings first stretched strings over wood to make sound, there's been a natural inclination to slide objects over the strings. In ancient India, musicians played an instrument called a gottuvadyam by gliding a small rod over the strings. But musicologists generally concur that the steel guitar was devised by Hawaiian schoolboy Joseph Kekuku, circa 1885. What makes it a "steel guitar" is that it's played with a metal bar like the one Kekuku made in his seventh-grade shop class. In the beginning, the guitars were just standard hollow body acoustics, played horizontally, with raised strings and thumb and finger picks. Hawaiian steel guitar became a national rage at 1915's Panama-Pacific International Exposition, which ran for seven months in San Francisco. The Hawaii legislature approved

$100,000 ($2 million today) to build a pavilion, which featured a giant aquarium, tropical flowers from floor to ceiling, statues of surfers, and the Hawaiian Quartette, featuring steel guitar and ukulele. This group outdrew a John Philip Sousa concert. America was captivated by the island culture.

In 1916, the Victor label alone released 140 recordings of Hawaiian music, many from Tin Pan Alley songwriters with nonsense Hawaiian choruses.

The most influential Hawaiian steel player was Sol Hoopii, the youngest in a family of twenty-one children on Oahu. "Some of the first Western swing steel players were copying Sol Hoopii note for note," said musician and ethnomusicologist Bob Brozman, who passed away in 2013. "He had a jazzman's instincts, and in the late '20s, early '30s he took the steel guitar places it had never gone before." Steel player Jerry Byrd, who left steady Nashville session work for the lounges of Waikiki in 1972, has said that Hoopii possessed the most dexterous picking hand he'd ever heard. Country music pioneer Jimmie Rodgers started hiring steel players from Hawaii in 1928 and popularized the "crying" accompaniment with country audiences. Bob Dunn of the Fort Worth-based Milton Brown and His Musical Brownies was among the first to play electric lap steel guitar in a country band, and Leon McAuliffe's hit 1936 recording of "Steel Guitar Rag" secured the instrument in the country music lexicon.

Remington's Ride

Also coming under the spell of Hawaiian music was a twelve-year-old kid from South Bend, Indiana, named Herb Remington. "There was just this huge Hawaiian craze, and the first time I heard that sound of a steel guitar, I thought, boy I gotta play me one of those," said Remington, a longtime Houstonian who passed away in 2018 at age ninety-two. Remington took lessons, at $1.25 each, from the Oahu Publishing Co., which had dispatched teachers and sheet music salesmen from Hawaii to points all over the country. "After you took thirty lessons, they gave you a little wooden guitar and a slide bar." The day after being discharged from the army in 1946, Remington auditioned for Bob Wills and became a Texas Playboy on the spot. He remained in the exalted band for four years before leaving to start a Hawaiian band, the Beachcombers, with his wife, Mel. After the Polynesian "exotica" fascination died down, the Remingtons opened a shop in Houston to build and sell both pedal and non-pedal steel guitars.

The Gibson guitar company came up with the "biscuit box on legs" design, which we currently identify with the steel guitar, in the late '30s. A few years later, pedals, knee levers, and multiple necks were added for more flexibility. But the complicated pedal steel guitar would not be embraced by Nashville until Bud Isaacs started playing it with Webb Pierce. "It was the big hit 'Slowly' in 1954," Remington recalled. "That's when the pedal steel guitar became THE thing. Every producer just had to have that pedal steel sound."

One of the best was Jimmy Day, who started out as a teenager on "the Louisiana Hayride" and backed Hank Williams and Elvis Presley on tour; then came long stints with Ray Price and Willie Nelson. Day was hanging out at the Sho-Bud showroom in Nashville one day in 1969 when a House of God bishop and his son, visiting from Rochester, New York, for a church convention, came in to look at the pedal steel guitars. The bishop asked Day to demonstrate one, and he used the half-pint whiskey bottle he'd been sipping on for a slide. He played "Amazing Grace," and tears welled up in Chuck Campbell's eyes. "It was the most beautiful thing I'd ever heard," Campbell recalled in 2007. Campbell watched the pedals, which allowed Day to switch tunings mid-song. Levers controlled by the knees raised and lowered the pitch. Suddenly, a whole new world of options opened up to the thirteen-year-old frontman of the Campbell Brothers. Switching to a pedal steel and exploring eerie tunings, Chuck forever changed his church's music.

But religious slide guitar had been pioneered decades earlier by Blind Willie Johnson, who was looking for more colors and more shading, and sliding up and down the strings gave him that. It's all around the edges of the frets, the darkness of the night, the cold firmness of the ground. That's where the passion is.

Gant
singingkeptussohappy
Family
Thesingingkeptussohappy
Singers

PART 2
Folk and Country

CHAPTER 7

The Families Lomax and Gant

"You Can't Kill a Culture"

It sure seemed quiet for 10 a.m. on a weekday, when John A. Lomax, who recorded folk songs for the Library of Congress, knocked on the front door of a six-room shanty on the northern bank of the Colorado River. Maggie Gant answered in her bedclothes. The children were still asleep, the mother of eight whispered.

"Last night we all got to singing and dancing. We didn't go to bed until two in the morning," she told Lomax, which he recalled in *Our Singing Country*, his 1941 book with son Alan that contained four songs collected from the Gants. "The singing kept us so happy, we couldn't go to sleep."

It was 1934, during the depths of the Depression, but the Gant family of dispossessed sharecroppers was rich in music. Lomax, a former University of Texas administrator, and nineteen-year-old Alan made more than forty primitive recordings of the family, whose repertoire ranged from jailhouse ballads and play ditties to cowboy songs and minstrel tunes. "The Gant family in Austin, Texas, has a repertoire of about two hundred genuine folk-songs," John Lomax wrote in a note found in the Lomax family papers, archived at UT's Center for American History. "We had only just begun the job of recording these tunes when we left town."

The most prominent of those, in retrospect, was "When First Unto This Country a Stranger I Came," which Joan Baez and Bob Dylan sang live, and Jerry Garcia and David Grisman recorded in 1993. They all learned it from the 1960s folkies the New Lost City Ramblers, who heard it from the Gants.

Mike Seeger (Pete's half-brother) of the Ramblers and his sister Peggy knew the song growing up, as their mother, Ruth Crawford Seeger, transcribed and archived the songs the Lomaxes recorded for the Library of Congress in the 1930s.

If Maggie Gant and her seventeen-year-old daughter, Foy, hadn't sung the tragic song about a jilted lover-turned-horse thief into the Lomax phonograph disk recorder, it almost certainly would've been lost forever.

ELLA

Based in Austin, the Lomaxes lived to keep such songs of the working-class people alive, road-tripping to prison work camps, Cajun settlements, fishing villages, cattle ranches, the hills of Kentucky, the Rio Grande Valley, and even Haiti to find words and music that told the story of the indigenous people. "You can't kill a culture," Alan once wrote, "until you kill the last person who cares about it."

With the Gant family of singers, led by mother Maggie (father George wasn't very musical), the Lomaxes found a treasure in their own backyard.

But John and son Alan left Austin in 1936 to manage and tour with their great discovery Leadbelly. Even with the Lomaxes recording only about 20 percent of their material, the Gant family left a body of work that puts them as "among the most important informants on traditional music that no one's ever heard of," said Minnesota musician/folklorist Lyle Lofgren. "The Gant family's list of songs passed down was astoundingly broad. It included many rare versions of archaic British ballads, the sort you might expect to find, if you were lucky, in some remote holler of the Appalachians, but probably not in Austin."

Where did this family of Mormons, originally from East Texas, learn some extremely rare songs of so many different styles? A clue came with the family's recently discovered genealogy, which daughter Foy Gant Kent registered with the Mormon church before she died in Houston in 2008 at age ninety. Maggie Gant's maternal grandmother, Lavinia "Lucy" Brown, was born in Wales, "the Land of Song," which has a rich ballad tradition. She moved to Tennessee, where Maggie's mother Sarah Reeves was born, then followed her to Texas, where Maggie was born in the town of Lone Oak in 1893. Lavinia Brown, the Welsh wellspring from which the songs most likely came, died in Grayson County, about sixty miles north of Dallas, when Maggie was six.

Austin's First Family of Song

The Gant family's path to Austin can be charted according to where the children were born, starting with oldest son Nephi in the northeast Texas town of Mineola in 1913. The next four—Ether, Foy, Adoniron and Ella—were born just a few miles south of Mineola, when the family lived in Kelsey, the largest Mormon colony in the state.

Georgia came next in Altus, Oklahoma, in 1925, and the youngest, Trovesta Mae, was born in 1929 in the Texas Panhandle town of Shamrock.

George, Maggie, and the kids arrived in Austin in 1933 looking for work and, according to Lomax, went on relief at times. The family lived in the riverside shack where the recordings were made, about a half-mile west of Deep Eddy Pool.

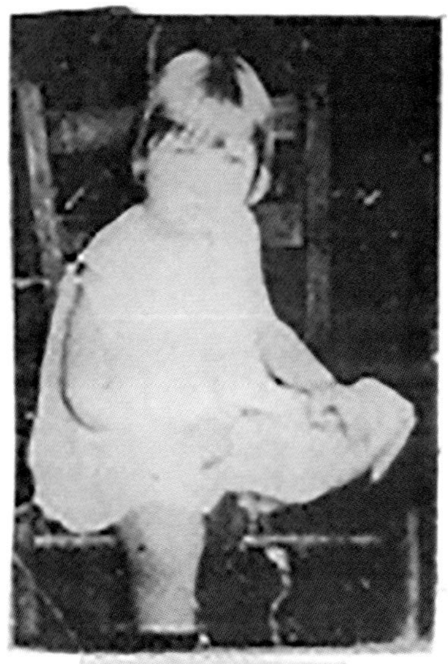

TROVESTA

Leadbelly

In her 2008 memoir *Sing It Pretty*, Alan's sister Bess Lomax Hawes, who was twelve when she met the Gants, recalled that the family's house on the river was constantly being flooded. "But that old river never could stop the flow of their extraordinary repertory of Anglo-American balladry and folksong."

The Gants recorded only for the Lomaxes, in four sessions spread out over two years. When World War II hit, the Gant family split between Houston, where there were jobs in the Ship Channel, and San Angelo, where the parents moved with their three youngest. Maggie and the kids never recorded together again after 1936.

But Austin's first family of song didn't stop singing. Maggie's grandson Edward Gant recalls Friday night folk song sessions in Houston led by Foy and her brothers Ether and Ado, as Adoniron was called. "There was music at every family gathering," said Ether's son Edward, who owns a Houston architectural firm.

Tim Gadd of Houston has a box full of cassettes of his grandfather Ado, who died in 2005 at age eighty-four, singing and playing the guitar. Several of the recordings feature duets with Ado and Ether, who both worked as welders and married sisters. But after Ether died in a 1977 car accident, Ado mainly recorded himself playing along with singers on TV.

The Lomax Legacy

The Lomax family background—patriarch John got his master's degree in the arts from Harvard University—was different from the Gants', but they had the Great Depression in common.

The Lomaxes operated under the idea of "cultural equity," that music made on a street corner in Marlin or a shack on the river was as valid as that of the world's great symphonies. The Lomax family dedicated their lives trying to restore the balance that wealth and privilege had taken away.

Although he made his mark as a folklorist with his 1910 songbook *Cowboy Songs and Other Frontier Ballads*, John Lomax had moved on to other pursuits and was working for a bank in Dallas during the 1929 stock market crash, which left him unemployed. Even worse, his wife Bess died in 1931, leaving him with two school-age children to raise. Alan was sixteen; Bess was nine.

Oldest son John Jr. encouraged his father, then sixty-five, to get back into "ballad hunt-

John Lomax
documentwhat
documentwhat
documentwhat
documentwhat
begin...
youhear
youhear
youhear
youhear
Henry Lebermann
Virginia Lebermann

MAMA & NEPHI

ing," a passion born from the cowboy songs Lomax heard growing up on a ranch in Bosque County, about forty miles north of Waco. In 1933, John started collecting songs for the Library of Congress and was named the head curator of its Archive of American Folk Songs.

The next year, John Sr. married Ruby Terrill, the dean of female students at UT. But just a few days later, John and Alan were on the road from Austin, getting permission to collect songs at the Clemmons Prison Farm outside Brazoria and state penitentiaries at Huntsville and Richmond. "My father figured that the sinners were probably in prison, so that's where we went to find their stories," Alan Lomax said in 1991.

The Lomaxes hit the trail and kept going. In June 1934, father and son would make their first foray to the Cajun and Creole regions of south central Louisiana. Aside from some records made in the 1920s by Leo Soileau and Amede Ardoin, the French-speaking black and white people of rural Louisiana were barely known outside the state. Alan knew a little French and father John was busy writing his memoirs, so this was really Alan's project. He was most excited by the *jure* style they found in Jennings, Louisiana, which sounded African in origin. The hand-clapping polyrhythms of *jure* would evolve into the infectious zydeco beat in the 1950s.

The summer of '34 in Louisiana was a major juncture in Alan Lomax's life, as he wrote that he "had my first glass of wine, my first shrimp creole, my first full-blown love affair and made my first independent field recordings." For part of the sojourn he was joined by his girlfriend Becky Machanofsky, a Russian-born Jewish social worker—and avowed Communist—he met in Austin. Becky urged Alan to break free from his father and move with her to Brooklyn. They soon split up.

The Library of Congress provided the Lomaxes with a 350-lb recording machine, which fit into the family's Ford after the back seats were removed. Superior to the old wax cylinder recorders John Lomax used to collect trail songs in the early 1900s, the new machine cut grooves onto a disk as the songs were sung, giving the singers a thrill when Lomax played back the record they'd just made.

In 1937, they drove to Eastern Kentucky and recorded a sixteen-year-old miner's daughter singing about a bordello: "There is a house in New Orleans/ They call the Rising Sun/ It's been the ruin of many a poor girl/ And God I know I'm one." When the Animals had the first "folk-rock" hit with "House of the Rising Sun" in 1964, Alan Lomax worked to see that Georgia Turner, then forty-three and destitute, receive at least a sliver of the royalties. She didn't write the old folk song, originally known as "Rising Sun Blues," but her version became the standard.

Tragedy Strikes "a Lovin' Bunch of Poor People"

According to John Lomax biographer Nolan Porterfield, the Lomaxes became aware of the Gants through budding folklorist John Henry

TROVESTA, ELLA & GEORGIA

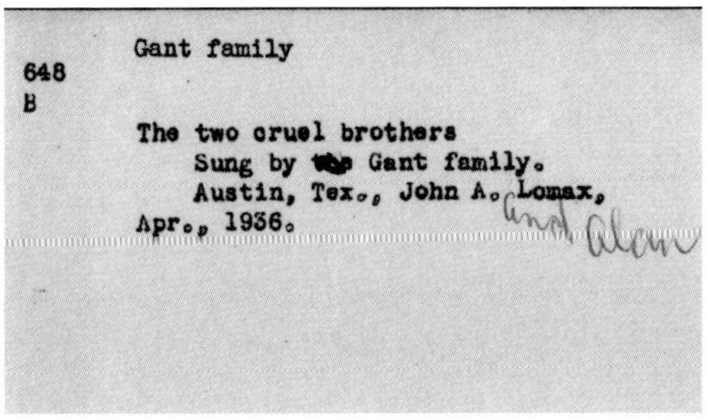

Gant family
648
B

The two cruel brothers
Sung by the Gant family.
Austin, Tex., John A. Lomax, and Alan
Apr., 1936.

Faulk, then a twenty-one-year-old UT classmate of Alan Lomax. Soon the Gants were starting to become well known to many in the Austin area and proudly accepted an invitation to play at the State's Centennial Celebration in Dallas in 1936.

But earlier that year, tragedy hit the singing family hard. Oldest boy Nephi, twenty-two, was murdered on February 1 after a fight at Ollie's Place at the corner of East Fourth and Waller Streets in East Austin.

According to a never-published story by Alan Lomax, Nephi, who had two hungry babies at home, had gone to the beer joint to try to borrow money from a bartender friend or "maybe he could pick up a few nickels singing . . . because he was the best singer in the family."

At Ollie's, Nephi was challenged to fight by a man who'd gotten out of prison just twenty-four hours earlier and was "already crazy drunk and looking for trouble," according to Alan Lomax. Nephi got the best of twenty-one-year-old Howard Armstrong, who went out to his car, got a gun, and shot Nephi in the head through the glass door. Sporting a black eye, Armstrong turned himself in to police the next day and claimed self-defense.

But the jury deliberated less than an hour before convicting Armstrong and sentencing him to thirty years in prison.

At Nephi's funeral, Alan Lomax noted that the family "cried so much that their eyes and cheeks were red with salt burn." Calling the Gants "a lovin' bunch of poor people," Lomax wrote of the incredible pain they surely felt at losing a brother, a son.

"They knew what it was like to be hungry and cold and not have a place to call home; but they'd been strong under all this suffering and sorrow because they loved each other so much."

After her children's father, George, died in 1943, Maggie Gant remarried and eventually moved to Arizona, where she ran a trailer court. She died in 1977 in Houston and, according to Mormon records, is buried in the same cemetery in San Angelo as George Gant.

Lofgren, the Minnesota folklorist, said the Gant family singers had "arrived seemingly from nowhere and disappeared again, at least as far as the folk song community was concerned." In fact, only in recent months did most of the Gants' descendants discover the extent of the family's influence.

"For so many years we kinda thought that Grandma's stories about her family being recorded were, ya know, exaggerations, tall Texas tales," said Ella Gant's granddaughter Julie, who recently contacted the Library of Congress and was stunned to receive in the mail several discs of recordings made by her grandmother Ella's family. "Now we are wondering if all the other crazy stories are also true."

Spotlighted Singers

The Gant family, singers of old-time folk songs, will be featured performers at Austin's folk festival Friday night at West Austin park. The Gants have made a large number of folk song recordings for the Library of Congress collection being compiled by John A. and Alan Lomax. Shown in front of Mrs. George and Ether Gant; standing, left to right Fay, Glida and Ella Gant.

boarder there, enrolled in 1883 at age ten and graduating in 1894. At that time, the school was located at the University of Texas "Little Campus" in what is now known as the Arno Nowotny Building next to the Erwin Center. The current location was built in 1917 on seventy-three donated acres.

Disaster in Galveston

After graduation, Lebermann moved back to Galveston and then to nearby Alvin to become a farmer. Besides music, Lebermann had a lifelong passion for growing and tended a vibrantly colorful garden until his death from congestive heart failure at age sixty-eight.

In August 1900, a hurricane destroyed Galveston, killing Lebermann's father and brother Lee. According to a 1937 *Austin Statesman* article, Henry Lebermann and another blind farmer spent several days in Alvin with water up to their waists, with no food, abandoned by their hired hand.

With a heart heavy with grief, Lebermann went back to the place in Austin that had been his home, his musical training ground. But this time, he would be an educator and leader. Kristi Sprinkle, a historian of the school, found records that Lebermann gave a classical music recital at the school in January 1901 and lectured on the life and work of Chopin in March of that year.

The school orchestra he led was one of the finest in Austin and was hired in 1904 to play a concert at Central Christian Church welcoming new students to UT. There, a thirty-three-year-old Lebermann met an eighteen-year-old church member named Virginia Carrington, whose father, Leonidas, owned the prosperous L. D. Carrington and Co. retail business on Congress Avenue.

After a year's courtship, Henry and Virginia were married. Son Lowell Sr. was born in 1906, with daughters Virginia and Jeanne soon following. The Lebermann name remained prominent in Austin when Henry and Virginia's grandson Lowell Jr. became a city councilman in the '70s and a University of Texas regent in the '90s.

When he accepted UT's Distinguished Alumni Award in 2000, Lowell Jr., who was blinded after a shooting accident at age twelve, credited his grandmother with expanding his cultural curiosity. "I'd go by the studio behind her house, and she'd be beating a tom-tom, breathing deeply and chanting," he said. "How many grandmothers that you know do that sort of thing?"

A progressive thinker and painter who spent summers at the Taos, New Mexico, artist community (sometimes accompanied by Lady Bird Johnson) as early as the 1930s, Virginia Leberman (1886–1968) was new age before the term was coined. She also co-owned the successful Christianson-Leberman Photography business where she photographed Eleanor Roosevelt and Will Rogers, among many others.

"We are perhaps more properly balanced than most married people," Virginia Leberman told the *Dallas Morning News* in a 1925 profile of her husband with the headline "Blind Genius at State Capital." "Each approves so entirely of the actions of the other that there is no friction in our home."

Leon Payne and Fred Lowery

In returning to the School for the Blind, Henry Lebermann hoped to have the same impact on his charges as Edmund Ludwig, his favorite music teacher, had on him. One such student was Fred Lowery, a native of Palestine in East Texas who was blinded at age two by scarlet fever. Lowery came to the school in 1917 at age seven and took to the musical training with dreams of becoming a concert violinist.

In his autobiography, *Whistling in the Dark*, Lowery recalls a "long, fatherly talk" he had with Lebermann about the steep odds facing a blind classical musician. "Here at the Blind School we can make music together because we use a system designed for the sightless," Lowery quotes Lebermann (blind musicians received their cues from the tapping of the leader's baton). "Sighted musicians are trained in a different system. They play by sight, reading the score, watching the conductor. Their system and our system won't mix."

Although the reality check was discouraging, Lowery credited Lebermann with sending him on the path of working in big bands. Having noticed Lowery whistling around school, Lebermann asked him to stay after band rehearsal one day. "I think we could use your whistle in the orchestra." Lebermann said he heard tones that suggested Lowery could mimic the sound of a piccolo, which the orchestra didn't have. Lebermann craved a piccolo sound on the John Philip Sousa marches that were crowd favorites.

Lowery went on to a great career as a whistler, making his name in the 1930s with the Vincent Lopez Orchestra, whose arranger was a trombone player named Glenn Miller. Perhaps best known for whistling the theme to "Lassie" and his TV duets with Bing Crosby, Lowery was a virtuoso who perfected the double-note whistle and performed such complex material as "The William Tell Overture."

Seven years younger than Lowery was Leon Payne from the northeast Texas town of Alba, who entered the School for the Blind in 1922. Under the tutelage of Lebermann and other teachers, Payne became proficient in guitar, keyboards, trombone, and drums. Nicknamed "The Blind Hitchiker," Payne was once picked up by the Bob Wills band bus and joined His

Jack Rhodes in the motel studio, courtesy Buddy Rhodes

Texas Playboys for a short spell just three years after graduating in 1935.

Although Payne began his career as a performer, hitting No. 4 on the Billboard country singles chart with "I Love You Because" (written in 1948 for his wife Myrtie, whom he met at the blind school), he's best known today as a songwriter. He wrote big hits for Hank Williams ("They'll Never Take Her Love from Me"), Jim Reeves ("Blue Side of Lonesome"), Dean Martin ("You've Still Got a Place in My Heart"), Carl Smith ("You Are the One," later covered by Smith's daughter Carlene Carter), and many more. Elvis Presley recorded "I Love You Because" at his very first Sun Records session, but pop singer Al Martino had the biggest hit with it. The 1948 Payne composition "Lost Highway," which he wrote on the side of the road between rides, was not a hit for Hank, but it's become one of his defining songs, as well as the namesake of several books, a record label, and a 1997 David Lynch film.

Payne's stepbrother was fellow hit songwriter Jack Rhodes ("Satisfied Mind," "Silver Threads and Golden Needles"), and the pair had a band based in Mineola called the Lone Star Buddies. They gigged all over East Texas in the '40s and were regulars on The Louisiana Hayride. One of the last songs Payne wrote in 1968 was the novelty number "Psycho," originally recorded by Eddie Noack and covered by Elvis Costello, among others.

Payne died of cancer at age fifty-two in San Antonio in 1969 and was inducted into the Nashville Songwriters Hall of Fame the next year. But he received his greatest honor in 1971, with the LP *George Jones Sings the Great Songs of Leon Payne*.

Leon Payne and Fred Lowery were Lebermann's best-known students, but hundreds more got lessons not only in music, but in carrying themselves without regard to disability. As a conductor of music and life he led in the most meaningful way—by example.

Henry Lebermann was blind, but not before he saw his mother's native Paris as a six-year-old. In darkness he created his own "City of Light" in a town he loved.

CHAPTER 9

Milton Brown

The Edison of Western Swing

"It's the same ol' tune, fiddle and guitar, where do we take it from here?" An ol' honky tonk hero sang that in the '70s, but back in the early '30s, Milton Brown and Bob Wills were thinking the same thing. The singer and the fiddler worked together less than two years in the Light Crust Doughboys, but what they started afterwards, when they kept adding instruments and improvisation, came to be called Western swing.

Although Wills earned the "King of Western Swing" tag with four decades of dancehall-filling dominance to make cowboy jazz a Texas tradition, the innovator was Brown, whose Musical Brownies were the prototype Western swing band in 1932. Four years later he'd be dead and his former partner would carry the torch with an "Ah-ha!" holler.

Brown's smooth vocals brought the city to the country and, with the addition of pianist Fred "Papa" Calhoun, the Brownies converted the string band into a dance outfit, mixing the previously disparate styles of jazz, country, blues, and pop to fill the floors. The 2/4 "Milton Brown Beat" revolved around the mighty strike hand of tenor banjoist Ocie Stoddard, who was followed closely by standup bassist Wanna Coffman and Milton's little brother Derwood Brown on heavy rhythm guitar. Fiddler Jesse Ashlock handled the melody, while Calhoun brought such an air of improvisation that he was nicknamed "Papa" by Brown in reference to legendary jazz pianist Earl "Fatha" Hines.

The Musical Brownies would first record in April 1934, a year and a half before Wills and the Texas Playboys. And yet Wills was called "the first great amalgamator of American music" when he and the Playboys were inducted into the Rock and Roll Hall of Fame in 1999. Milton Brown is not even in the *Country* Music Hall of Fame!

Milton led the band for only four years, during the Depression, but he knew how to get the people to come out. The Musical Brownies were easily the most popular dance band in Texas in the early '30s, but they almost never played out of state, except to record in Chicago and New Orleans.

In Cary Ginell's oral history *Milton Brown and the Founding of Western Swing* (University of Illinois Press, 1994), Calhoun recalls being dragged out to Crystal Springs Dance Pavilion, four miles northwest of Fort Worth, on a snowy Thursday night in late '32 and being impressed by the turnout of hundreds for Milton and the boys. Billed as "the Colonel from Kentucky" (though he was from Chico, Texas), Calhoun played solo jazz piano on KTAT, so he was known to the Brownies, but nobody played keyboards with a string band back then. Milton removed the cover of the house piano and called Calhoun up to sit in on "Nobody's Sweetheart," and the pianist jammed for the entire set. During intermission he was asked to join the Brownies.

They had found something special, but Brown was not done assembling his dream lineup.

He hired classically trained Cecil Brower to play twin fiddle—a new concept—with Ashlock at first, then Cliff Bruner. In late '34 came steel guitar genius Bob Dunn, who started off as a Hawaiian-style player, then found greater satisfaction emulating the sliding trombone of Vernon's Jack Teagarden. But how could Dunn's guitar, a Martin acoustic laid flat and played with a steel bar, be heard over this hot band? With "Taking Off," recorded in Chicago in January 1935, Dunn had the distinction of being the first to record an electric guitar, played through a magnetic mic in the soundhole.

Brown developed the idea to play a jazz/pop repertoire with country music instrumentation, but Wills went bigger, adding drummer Smokey Dacus in 1935, then a horn section soon after. Wills and his thirteen-piece orchestra, with Brown's replacement Tommy Duncan on vocals, did not see themselves as competing with the Musical Brownies as much as with national swing orchestras on tour. Filling every square of air in the enormous dancehalls and ballrooms of Texas and Oklahoma, the Texas Playboys eventually outdrew Tommy Dorsey and Harry James. Like Milton, Bob could always get the top players, including slidemaster Leon McAuliffe, whose 1936 recording of "Steel Guitar Rag" was every bit as influential as Dunn's groundbreaking work.

Ginell identifies four eras of Western swing. The first is the advent of Milton and the Musical Brownies, and the second era is defined by the late '30s Tulsa residency of Bob Wills and the Texas Playboys, who broadcast daily from Cain's Ballroom on 50,000-watt KVOO. The Wills group maintained vitality through the next two eras, headed by Spade Cooley-Tex Williams in the '40s and Waco's Hank Thompson and the Brazos Valley Boys in the '50s. The term "Western swing" wasn't used until applied to Cooley, an Okie who had moved to California during the Dust Bowl. Trade magazines tried to call it "hillbilly jazz," but the h-word was considered derisive.

Wills is still the king because in April 1936, Milton Brown crashed his new Pontiac Silver Streak into a telephone pole on the Jacksboro Highway and was dead at thirty-three. Band members surmised, because they'd seen him do it before, that Brown fell asleep at the wheel (giving name to the longtime Western swing upholders of Ray Benson). His passenger, sixteen-year-old aspiring singer Katy Prehoditch, was killed instantly in the 3 a.m. crash. The recently divorced Brown died six days later of pneumonia while still in the hospital. His ex-wife Mary Helen married Bob Wills in 1938.

Milton and the Musical Brownies left a rich recorded legacy—sixteen sides for Bluebird in 1934, and over one hundred for Decca, recorded in the fifteen months before Brown's death. But live is where they really took off, with the dancers spurring them on. It's lucky for fans of Texas string band dance music that Wills and the Playboys were there to "take it away." There was an abundance of overshadowing, but if the Texas Playboys weren't so thrilling for so long, Brown's vision wouldn't have gone as far.

Like Wills, Milton Brown grew up in rural Texas (Stephenville) with a fiddle whiz as his pop. But Milton was a singer, not a player. Back then, the house party band would be a fiddler and a guitarist, and most tunes were instrumental. If there were vocals on fiddle music, they were country-raw, from the backwoods, while Brown's vocals were smooth, from the ballroom. Milton listened to country blues, Bessie Smith, Cab Calloway, and Bing Crosby, but with the old-time fiddle tunes part of his makeup, he had a mindset to meld.

Everybody wanted that swing, pioneered by the 1920s Fletcher Henderson Orchestra, with Louis Armstrong's trumpet peppering

It began with
Milton Brown
Western Swing original

and
Sippie Wallace
Charles Brown
Amos Milburn

PART 3

Rhythm and Blues

CHAPTER 10

Amos Milburn and Charles Brown

Ivory Ghosts

Fats Domino and Ray Charles are titans of American music, lauded as the architects of rock 'n' roll and soul music, respectively. And yet it was a pair of now-obscure Texans, a gay couple, it turns out, who showed them the way.

Amos loved his whiskey and Charles was a gambling fiend, so the Sportsman Club in Newport, Kentucky, just over the Ohio River from Cincinnati, was a place they could be together with their vices night after night. They also played and sang at the illegal casino, but it's not like they had a choice.

Charles especially had a problem with horses that wore numbers and little men, but you didn't borrow money from Frank "Screw" Andriola unless you had a "can't miss" tip. The only sure thing, however, ended up being a nightly appearance at the mobster's Sportsman Club for as long as it took to repay the debt. In August 1961, the gig neared the one-year mark.

That's the month Hilton Owens started hanging around the Sportsman, which catered to a black clientele. The first night he couldn't believe the lobby placard that said recording artists Charles Brown and Amos Milburn were playing in the lounge. These guys had number one hits! His job as an undercover Internal Revenue Service agent was to infiltrate and observe the gaming operations, but on hearing Milburn's "Chicken Shack Boogie," the first thing Owens investigated was where that fat groove was coming from. When Charles Brown sang "Black Night" the next set, the roulette tables could wait.

Brown's songs of romantic yearning were undoubtedly a boon to Andriola's bordello next door, while Milburn's sets spurred bar sales. He'd become so associated with drinking songs after "Bad, Bad Whiskey" topped the charts in 1950, followed by "Thinkin' and Drinkin'," "Let Me Go Home, Whiskey," and the original "One Scotch, One Bourbon, One Beer," that Amos lined shot glasses on the top of his upright when he played.

"You guys should be headlining at the Apollo!" Owens told the singing ivorysmiths during a break. It had been years since they'd had a hit, but Brown and Milburn were still in their thirties, with skills undiminished. One night, Owens approached Charles with a concerned look. "How long would it take you and Amos to get out of here?" As recounted in Owens's 2011 memoir *Three of the First*, the Sportsman was about to be raided as part of new Attorney General Robert Kennedy's war on mob-controlled activities. "I heard the axes hit the front door and we hid in the ceiling," Milburn recalled in a recently unearthed 1979 interview, conducted just nine months before his death of a heart attack at age fifty-two.

Charles and Amos looked down from the rafters on that night of August 22, 1961, to see Andriola being led away in handcuffs. Their forced residency was over! But where were they going to go tomorrow night?

At least the pair got a good song out of their dicey situation. In January '61, Brown and Milburn recorded "I Want To Go Back Home" as a duet for Cincy's King label. A Sportsman-inspired rewrite of an earlier single on Ace, the record didn't chart, but Sam Cooke dug it, which was just as good. The soul superstar wanted to re-record the number as a duet with Charles, but on the day of the 1962 session in Los Angeles, Brown went to the racetrack instead. Faced with a studio of musicians on the clock, Cooke changed most of the words into "Bring It On Home To Me" and leaned the melody just far enough to make it legally his own. Lou Rawls sang what would've been Brown's answer part on the classic.

You don't get famous for what you start and today Brown and Milburn, whose suave musicianship helped change the "race records" designation in the trades to the more honorable "rhythm and blues" in the late '40s, are much less known than who they inspired.

After Fats Domino took off from the Ninth Ward of New Orleans to the top of the R&B charts with his first single "The Fat Man" in 1950, he was routinely asked about his influences and acknowledged one name above the others. "I first heard (piano) triplets on an Amos Milburn record," Domino said in his 2006 biography *Blue Monday: Fats Domino and the Lost Dawn of Rock 'n' Roll*. The three-notes-to-a-beat sound he discovered on Milburn's 1947 record "Operation Blues" and became further fascinated with on Little Willie Littlefield's 1949 hit "It's Midnight," was refurbished on such hits as "Blueberry Hill," and would become a foundation of New Orle-

ans R&B, and therefore rock 'n' roll. Fats said Amos was "the only blues singer I tried to sing like," and he even hunched over the piano with a cherubic grin like his hero from Houston.

The model for a teenaged Ray Charles, meanwhile, was Charles Brown of Texas City, who helped define West Coast Blues with a brooding, yet always elegant style that spoke to African Americans hopeful for a better lifestyle after WWII. "Charles Brown was a powerful influence on me in the early part of my career, especially when I was struggling down in Florida," Ray Charles said in the bio *Brother Ray* by David Ritz. "I made many a dollar doing my imitation of his 'Drifting Blues.' That was a hell of a number."

Ironically, the intensified music of the protégés steamrolled the '78s of jumpin' and swayin' blues that had given them a jukebox education. Teenagers in the fifties were learning to live in the moment and had no use for the musicians who *anticipated* rock 'n' roll. Brown and Milburn both hit a cold streak in 1954, after "Rock Around the Clock" by Bill Haley and the Comets changed everything. From 1946 to 1953, Brown and Milburn had more than fifteen hit R&B singles each. After that they had none. Aladdin tried to make its former chart-toppers relevant again by booking them into Cosimo Matassa's hit factory in New Orleans in September 1956, backed by the musicians who played on those number ones by Domino and Little Richard. But the results were disappointing, financially, at least. Brown recorded eleven tracks in one day, but only three were released. Milburn re-cut "Chicken Shack Boogie" in the same session, but although the recording blows away almost anything else on the charts in '56, few heard it. "It was too fast for R&B and too slow for rock 'n' roll," Milburn reasoned of radio's rejection of the French Quarter version of his signature tune. You had to sing like your hair was on fire in 1956, and Charles and Amos were too cool for that.

One has to wonder if the music biz buzz about the Brown/Milburn relationship might've also had something to do with why they fell out of favor. It was known in their musical circle that Brown and Milburn were gay, confirmed in interviews by guitar players, an ex-wife and a manager/lawyer. "Various older musicians told us they were a couple," said guitarist Danny Caron, Brown's bandleader from 1987 until the pianist's 1999 death at age seventy-six. "But the public didn't know about it." Brown's manager Howell Begle, who worked for the estate until he died in January 2019 after a skiing accident, said in 2017 that he'd heard the pair of piano greats were together during the years they were on King Records, from 1960 to 1963. But he never heard that from Brown himself, only from musicians close to him. "Charles and I were very close and he never once talked about being gay," said Begle.

Brown's ex-wife Mabel Scott, herself a popular singer/pianist, was frank about her relationship with "the great love of my life" in an interview with RJ Smith for his 2006 book *The Great Black Way*. "He was a homosexual," she said of Brown, "and the men drove me crazy." The splashy showbiz wedding of 1949, which made the cover of *Ebony*, was the back page divorce of '51.

Milburn was outed by longtime Chickenshackers guitar player Texas Johnny Brown in a 1987 interview published in the book *Texas Blues*. "He was gay, but easy to get along with," said Brown, revealing a slight discomfort.

The gay relationship "wasn't a secret to us," said eighty-five-year-old blues belter Carol Fran, whose husband, esteemed Houston guitarist Clarence Holliman (1937–2000), played in Brown's band for many years. Everyone called Holliman "Gristle" after an infamous incident on the road with Brown. In a moment of misplaced lust one night, the singer went to grab the guitarist's crotch and had his hand slapped away. "Ah, man, it's just gristle," Brown remarked. Holliman embraced the nickname and played his blues bad to the bone.

Neither Brown nor Milburn ever publicly admitted to being gay because it just didn't make financial sense to ruin the fantasies of so many female record and ticket buyers. There was also the choice between the closet and the cell. Sexual activity between persons of the same gender was a criminal act in all states until the mid-1960s.

The pair came off as domestic partners in interviews, with Brown praising Milburn's dinner chops. "He made chitlins and neckbones and anything you wanted. I loved his way with food," Brown said in 1993, but later complained about his roommate's drinking. "Amos and I lived in the same apartment and he was out partying every night, acting like the world was coming to an end," said Brown, who drank only rarely.

Brown and Milburn's close association goes back to 1946, when Charles was ridin' high with "Drifting Blues" and Amos, just back from the war, was the new boogie-woogie prince of Houston. "Charles was an admirer of mine even before I moved to L.A.," Amos told bluesologist Charlie Lange. When he sang blues ballads, it was obvious Milburn also looked up to Brown.

The eighth of twelve children and the first born in Texas to Louisiana natives, Amos was a natural on the piano from first reach and tinkle. His musician brother Frederick, older by twelve years, showed him things, and it just took off from there. No church for young Amos, who found his religion hanging outside Third Ward juke joints in the late '30s.

According to the liner notes of Mosaic's 1994 set *The Complete Aladdin Recordings of Amos Milburn*, the piano prodigy had an early act billed "He-Man Martha Raye," performing novelty numbers he'd heard the comedic hoofer sing in movies like 1941's *Navy Blues*. Raye joined the USO in 1942, and in November of that year a fifteen-year-old Amos became seventeen on his paperwork and enlisted in the Navy. He was assigned to the food crew of a ship based in the Philippines, and it's not known if Seaman Milburn ever met "The Big Mouth," but you can be sure he entertained the fellas with his Martha routine. And he certainly had access to a piano, because just a

month after returning to Houston from the Navy in October '45 to attend Amos Sr.'s funeral (pneumonia), he was playing Sid's Ranche chicken shack in Houston backed by the house band. Six months later Milburn opened for T-Bone Walker at Don Robey's Bronze Peacock.

The big three of boogie-woogie piano—Pete Johnson, Albert Ammons, and Meade Lux Lewis—were big influences on Milburn, as were jazz pianist Art Tatum, R&B great Louis Jordan, and Nashville's Cecil Gant, "the G.I. Sing-sation," who also moved between ballads and boogie-woogie. But the most significant musical moment of his life as a listener, he's said, came when his ship pulled into the harbor at Long Beach, California, at the end of WWII, and the radio picked up "Blues at Sunrise" by Ivory Joe Hunter. It was a new day on the coast, and Milburn heard a world he wanted to be part of. Backing Kirbyville, Texas, native Hunter on the smooth and lowdown 1945 recording were Johnny Moore's Three Blazers with Charles Brown playing that sly, sparkling piano that Amos took right to his heart.

West Coast Blues, Texas Style

African American musicians from Texas didn't flock to Memphis or Chicago; they went to South Central LA, Harlem with palm trees. They brought the heavy blues and gospel feel from home, refining it with inventive instrumentation and smooth vocals. In the mid-1930s blues guitarists T-Bone Walker from Dallas, Rockdale's Pee Wee Crayton, and Austin-born Johnny Moore came looking for more opportunities in a relaxed racial climate. The '40s saw the migration of piano men, including Floyd Dixon of Marshall, plus tenor saxmen Illinois Jacquet, Don Wilkerson of Houston, and Joe Houston from Bastrop. Songwriter Jessie Mae Robinson, who wrote #1 hits for Brown ("Black Night") and Milburn ("Roomin' House Boogie," "In the Middle of the Night"), as well as the rockabilly classic "Let's Have a Party" for Wanda Jackson, was originally from Jasper. Others finding success out west were Esther Phillips of Galveston, Peppermint Harris from Texarkana, Little Willie Littlefield from El Campo, and first choice bassist Shifty Henry (immortalized in the lyrics of "Jailhouse Rock") from Edna. Nat Cole, from Chicago, was still the King on the LA club scene, but even he had an essential Texan, Johnny Moore's younger brother Oscar Moore, who crafted the small-combo jazz guitar style during his ten years (1937-47) with the King Cole Trio.

Charles Brown made it to LA in late '44 and quickly drew notice on Central Avenue by winning a talent show at the Lincoln Theater with a wry segue of Earl Hines's "Boogie with St. Louis Blues" into "Warsaw Concerto." Brown, who'd been a high school science teacher in Texas just a year prior, proved to be the kind of cultured bluesman that Central Avenue was looking for. He was hired on the spot to play piano at Ivie's Chicken Shack (ironically, an upscale joint), where he rotated with his best friend from Prairie View A&M (class of '42) Richie Dell Archia. The sister of noted jazz saxman Tom Archia, Richie got Charles that teaching job at Carver High in Baytown right out of college because her father was the principal. But sheer talent is what opened the doors for Brown in the music field.

Johnny Moore was in the audience at the Lincoln the night Brown dazzled on those piano instrumentals. His band was a Blazer short, needing a piano player who could handle lead vocals, so Moore tracked down Brown, who was working during the day as an elevator operator at a department store. Asked to audition, the pianist said he wasn't a vocalist. But Charles gave it a try, singing 1941 hit "Embraceable You" by his favorite singer Helen O'Connell. The Blazers were three again and went to work right away, making music that made babies.

Milburn was discovered at San Antonio's Keyhole Club in the summer of '46 by Lola Ann Cullum, the fifty-year-old wife of a prominent Houston dentist. Active in Houston black society, the Cullums made the *Houston Informer* front page when they put up W. C. Handy, "Father of the Blues," in March 1946. The visit seemed to have strengthened musical aspirations in Lola Ann, whose life of transitions began when she went from Weimar farm girl to the Alpha Kappa Alpha sorority at Howard University circa 1914. Cullum trekked to the Keyhole, a 350-capacity former movie theater

at the corner of Pine and Iowa Streets, that summer night to see Duke Ellington. Way down on the bill was Milburn, who played his own set and backed the brother-sister dance team of Mack & Ace. "When you come back to Houston," Cullum told nineteen-year-old Milburn, "let's make some recordings." Lola Ann had just bought a Soundmirror tape recorder, the first available to the public, and was eager to get in on the postwar R&B explosion.

Cullum had a slow blues tune she'd been messing around with called "After Midnight," which Milburn finished on the Cullum's baby grand piano and sang in the style of Charles Brown. The demo, recorded on paper-backed magnetic tape, appealed to the Mesner brothers, Leo and Eddie, who had the hit with "Drifting Blues" when their LA label was called Philo. They were looking for the next Charles Brown, but what the renamed Aladdin Records signed was the most-rockin' piano player on the scene. Milburn's roadhouse romper "Down the Road Apiece," from the maiden Milburn session in September 1946, got the juices flowing like a first kiss. When Chuck Berry covered the tune in 1960, Milburn's record was the source, not the tamer 1940 original by the Will Bradley Trio (featuring Fort Worth's Ray McKinley on drums).

Keyhole Club and Mrs. Cullum

The significance of Don Albert's Keyhole Club goes beyond being the launching pad for the careers of Milburn and Clarence "Gatemouth" Brown. What set the Keyhole apart from others in the "Chitlin' Circuit" of raucous Southern juke joints was that it was integrated—on the bandstand and in the crowd—and had been since the first location opened in November 1944 on the Eastside. Drawing clientele from military bases in and around San Antonio, owner Albert and his backer Willie "Red" Winner advertised that all races were welcome at the Keyhole, then had to go to the Texas Supreme Court to fight a racist police commissioner intent on closing them down.

The original Keyhole closed in 1948, reopening at 1619 W. Poplar Street in 1950. What happened in between was that President Harry Truman ordered the US Armed Forces desegregated, which had a rippling effect in military-heavy San Antonio. The new Keyhole found a growing clientele of white soldiers and airmen crazy for R&B, who found out about the place from their black base-mates. While only a smattering of whites, including sax player Zoot Simms, went to the original Keyhole, which was in a black neighborhood, the second location would sometimes have as many whites inside as blacks.

Not everyone was in favor of such race-mixing, especially when the cause of congregation was the frenzied beat of African American "devil music." The thought of white women dancing with black men infuriated those who wanted to maintain white supremacy.

Newly elected fire and police commissioner George M. Roper made it his mission to shut down the sinful Keyhole after he took his post in May 1951. Roper was a war hero who spent 1942-45 in a Japanese POW camp. He was also a rabid segregationist, who aimed S. A.'s vice squad at the club. Just a month into Roper's term the Keyhole was raided after midnight, and more than three hundred patrons were arrested on curfew and liquor violations. More than a hundred of those were servicemen, who were handed over to military police. The rest went to jail, where they were released after paying a $5 fine.

Until the Civil Rights Act of 1964, there were laws that allowed white-owned businesses to deny service and access to blacks, but there was nothing authorities could do to legally prevent whites from entering black-owned businesses. So Roper and his men turned to harassment. One night the cops burst in during the Keyhole's floor show, which often included one-legged tap dancer Peg Leg Bates and "Iron Jaws," whose act was dancing with a table between his teeth, and ordered the crowd to stand and be counted. Another night, officers seized thirty cases of beer when it was discovered that Winner owned a liquor store. Texas law prohibited an individual who owned a package store to also have a beer and wine permit.

Citing a faulty roof, without any input from city code inspectors, Roper ordered the Keyhole closed on June 22, 1951. But Albert and Winner had hired attorney Van Henry Archer, Sr., who filed a temporary restraining order so the Keyhole could stay open until the case went to court.

In October 1951, Associate Justice Jack Pope of the Texas Supreme Court ruled in the Keyhole's favor, blasting Roper's action as "not due process of law. It is no process at all." The restraining order became permanent, plus Pope ordered the police commissioner and other city officials to pay all court costs. The Keyhole Club, the western point of the Chitlin' Circuit, was officially recognized as the first integrated nightclub in the south.

Albert sold the club in 1964, and it closed soon after. The end of segregation wiped out the Chitlin' Circuit. The bigger acts could play larger capacity venues previously denied. And music fans could now go to any venue in town.

Don Albert, who recorded eight sides for Vocalion Records with his Ten Pals swing band in November 1936 as part of the same sessions that produced Robert Johnson's first recordings, went back to playing music after he sold the second and final Keyhole. The respected elder of the San Antonio jazz scene (who maintained his 1936 sessions were recorded at the Bluebonnet Hotel, not the historically embraced Gunther) died at age seventy-two in 1980.

After Milburn, "Mrs. Cullum," as everyone called her, brought her next discovery Lightnin' Hopkins to Aladdin in November '46, and went two-for-two as a talent scout when Hopkins hit the Top Ten in 1949 with "T-Model Blues." A female manager in the 1940s was rare, indeed, and Cullum no doubt met with prejudice. But she was sharp, educated, and connected, and she used maternal instincts to get the most out of her acts and those who could benefit them. A "hands on" rep, she bought Milburn's clothes and helped him and Aladdin staff producer/saxophonist Maxwell Davis choose the songs to record. But when Cullum's management contract was up for renewal in 1949, the Mesners convinced Milburn he was too hot for her to handle. After a failed attempt at starting a record label in Houston, Don Robey's turf, a heartbroken Cullum went back to being a dentist's wife full time. The yearly, dwindling royalty checks as cowriter of "Chicken Shack Boogie" and "Hold Me Baby" were all she had to show for her time in the music biz.

The Thomas Family and the Roots of Boogie-Woogie

"Gonna Have a Real Booga-Rooga Tonight"

Just as Milburn moved on from Mrs. Cullum, he left boogie-woogie behind for a smoother R&B sound. But that style of music, with the heavy left hand mimicking the choogle of steam locomotives while the right played melodic cross-rhythms that whistled up and down the tracks, was the foundation of Texas blues piano. Amos never forgot that.

Boogie-woogie was a national craze during WWII; then it evolved into rock 'n' roll the next decade. But its roots, according to oral histories, can be traced to East Texas logging camps in the 1870s, when former slaves were drawn to the more percussive properties of the piano to get the people dancing. With all their workers now free to walk away from hard labor, the lumber companies built "barrelhouses" to keep the men from straying into town, and also to get back that paycheck money.

Before Clarence Smith gave it a name with "Pine Top's Boogie Woogie" in 1929, the eight-beats-to-the-bar gyration generator was called "Fast Texas" or "Fast Western." Untutored ivorysmiths rode the rails of the Texas Western from camp to camp, finding work in those makeshift juke joints where they kept the booze in barrels. "Boogie-woogie came out of wherever there were black people," Honey Grove pianist Sammy Price succinctly put it in *The Jazz Scene*. "Blind Lemon Jefferson used to play those movements on his guitar and they called it 'booga-rooga.'" (Price discovered the much-older Jefferson while working at R. T. Ashford's record store in Deep Ellum and recommended him to Paramount Records.) The term came to describe parties and then became attached to the music that inspired the wildest ones.

A pair of Texas brothers, whose father George Thomas Sr. worked for the Southern Pacific Railroad and was a deacon at Shiloh Baptist Church, are credited with taking the left-handed "walking bass" figure nationally. George W. Thomas Jr. and younger brother Hersal's sheet music for "The Fives" in 1922 and "The Rocks" in '23 legitimized boogie-woogie. A cover of George Jr.'s "Muscle Shoals Blues" was Fats Waller's very first recording for OKeh in 1922. "The world wants dancing music, and, tunefulness apart, wants something not reminiscent of hundreds of dances that have gone before," George Jr. told the *Music Trade Review*, which noted how "Muscle Shoals" sounded unique.

With sisters Beulah "Sippie" Wallace and Hociel Thomas (actually George Jr.'s daughter but raised as a sister) having hit blues records on OKeh in the '20s, the Thomases have to be considered "The First Family of Texas Music." They also helped raise "Moanin'" Bernice Edwards, a fantastic piano player who recorded for Paramount in the late '20s and ARC in the early '30s.

After a time bouncing between Houston and New Orleans, where George Jr. wrote the highly influential twelve-bar "New Orleans Hop

Scop Blues" in 1912 or so, the Thomas Brothers moved to Chicago around 1921. Sippie and her second husband Matt Wallace followed, with "The Texas Nightingale" signing to OKeh in 1923 and having big hits with "Shorty George Blues," "Mighty Tight Woman," and "Women Be Wise," which Bonnie Raitt would resurrect in 1971. In the '60s, Canned Heat put the lyrics of Sippie's "Up the Country Blues," with the music of "Bulldoze Blues" by Henry Thomas of Big Sandy, to have a huge hit with "Going Up the Country" (without crediting Wallace or Thomas).

George Jr., who said he was missing half his right thumb in a 1918 draft registration card, handled the publishing and wrote songs, while teenaged piano prodigy Hersal, twenty-one years his junior, hit the theaters and juke joints and demonstrated the tunes. After recording "Suitcase Blues" under his own name in 1925, Hersal backed Hociel, who by this time he knew was his niece, not his sister (unless Hersal, born two years after Hociel, was also secretly George's child) on sessions with Louis Armstrong on cornet that yielded "Deep Water Blues" and "Lonesome Hours."

After Sippie and Matt moved to Detroit, Hersal followed and got a gig at Penny's Pleasure Inn in June 1926. But that engagement turned tragic when Hersal got suspected food poisoning and died a week later. He was only nineteen.

Clarence Smith was shot to death in a Chicago dance club in 1929, just a month after "Pine Top's Boogie Woogie" became a smash hit. Others capitalized for him, with Dallas barrelhouse player Whistlin' Alex Moore releasing his first LP on Columbia that year, plus Will Ezell of Brenham putting out his most popular singles "Barrelhouse Woman," "Helter Dust,"

and "Playing the Dozens." But it was quickly over. Ezell ended the year escorting the body of fellow Paramount recording artist Blind Lemon Jefferson back to Wortham for burial.

Sippie's grief over her youngest brother's death sent her back to church and obscurity, where she was the organist at Leland Baptist Church in Detroit for forty years. At the urging of lifelong friend Victoria Spivey, Wallace returned to public performance during the 1960's folk/blues revival. She performed right up until her death in 1986 at age eighty-eight, often with a beaming Raitt by her side.

Hociel Tebo, her married name, had a brief return to the music business in 1946 after being tracked down in Oakland by jazz promoter Rudi Blesh, who signed her to his Circle label. "Tebo's Texas Boogie" shows Hociel's rollicking piano skills undiminished, and she joined Kid Ory's band as singer. But "Tragedy Mars Comeback of a Former Blues Star," as *downbeat* headlined in late 1949, when Hociel shot and killed Queen O. Smith, forty-three, after a drag-out fight that started as an argument between Hociel's preteen daughters over how to fix their hair. Mrs. Tebo told police Mrs. Smith was her sister, but they had different parents and weren't raised together. After spending a couple months in jail, Hociel was acquitted on the grounds of self-defense. She died of a heart attack in 1952 at age forty-eight.

The "walking bass" fever did not become an epidemic until 1938, when Pete Johnson, Albert Ammons, and Meade Lux Lewis played John Hammond's "Spirituals to Swing" concert at Carnegie Hall. Although George Thomas Jr. had died the previous year at age fifty-three, he and Hersal were noted in the Carnegie Hall program: "Albert Ammons and Meade 'Lux' Lewis claim that 'The Fives,' the Thomas brothers' musical composition, deserves much credit for the development of modern boogie woogie. During the twenties, many pianists featured this number as a 'get off' tune and in the variations played what is now considered boogie-woogie. This is the first appearance in print of this composition."

Alan Lomax recorded Johnson, Ammons, and Lewis in New York City the day after the sensational Carnegie Hall performance, which would've stolen the show if Sister Rosetta Tharpe, Big Joe Turner, and the Count Basie Orchestra weren't also on the historic bill.

Moon Mullican and the Birth of Rock 'n' Roll Piano

The most direct link between boogie-woogie and rock 'n' roll was through a white barrelhouse pianist from the Piney Woods, Corrigan's Aubrey "Moon" Mullican, who was the primary influence on Jerry Lee Lewis. With those rollicking country blues records Mullican recorded for King Records in the late '40s and barnstorming Texas-Louisiana tours with his Showboys, he was dubbed "The King of the Hillbilly Piano" without any real contenders. The former Texas Wanderers singer also delivered warm, soulful vocals with a country drawl. He cowrote "Jambalaya (On the Bayou)," according to several accounts, but had a bad publishing deal so he sold it outright to Hank Williams. Portly and balding, Mullican didn't have the superstar look, but his talent and influence are undeniable.

Also based in Houston in 1946, Mullican had no doubt heard about Amos Milburn, that young black R&B piano player just back in town from the navy, who also made the beer bottles bounce on tabletops. Both had hot bands and made their recording debuts in September 1946, but race divided the men as if they lived on separate coasts. There's no evidence that the first two great pianists of rock 'n' roll ever met.

Amos Milburn got wrapped up in the WWII boogie-woogie craze while in the navy and recorded two piano romps at that first session. To give it some grease, Milburn scat-hummed over his lightning right hand, while his left kept a furious beat. Boogie-woogie had been popular for years, but no one had heard it played as emphatically, with ghost tinkles, as Milburn on "Down the Road Apiece" and "Amos' Boogie."

While Lightnin' went back to Houston, Amos had found his paradise in LA. He was named #1 R&B jukebox artist of 1949, at age twenty-one, landing four singles—"Chicken Shack Boogie," "Bewildered," "Hold Me Baby," and "Roomin' House Boogie"—on the list of the thirty most-played '78s of the year. Milburn repeated as jukebox champ in 1950, with Charles Brown taking the top spot the next year, with the haunting "Black Night" spending fourteen weeks at #1.

In a race to find the next Amos Milburn, Modern's Jules Bihari flew to Houston in 1949 and caught a raucous set by a teenaged Little Willie Littlefield at the Eldorado Ballroom. Bihari signed Littlefield, who had Top 5 R&B hits with "It's Midnight" and "Farewell," but is most notable today for being the first to record the Lieber-Stoller classic "Kansas City" in 1952 for Federal Records. Label A&R head Ralph Bass changed the title to "K.C. Loving" to sound hipper, but when Wilbert Harrison covered it in 1959 as its original title, he had a #1 song.

Aladdin's Shining Stars

Aladdin was one of the big four independent R&B labels on the West Coast after WWII—along with Modern, Imperial, and Specialty—and Milburn and Brown were its biggest stars. Both were sensational piano players, but their music was two sides of the R&B coin, with Milburn's joviality the flip of Brown's entrancing melancholy. Charles was classically trained; Amos couldn't read music. But they were both bluesmen and a natural pairing on their constant co-headliner tours, creating a range of moods.

"The first night me and the boys played the Apollo, the crowd was wondering 'what are these Texas cowboys gonna do up there?'" Milburn recalled in 1979. "The curtains parted, we came on to 'Chicken Shack Boogie' and it looked like the roof was gonna blow off!" The most fun joints are generally the most dangerous, was the song's message, and it went over big in Harlem. Milburn had played enough chicken shacks in Outskirts, Texas, to have seen it all by a young age.

Charles Brown kept his piano blues in a more laid back, swankier locale. Matinee idol handsome, with a voice like a dark, lingering

Moon
Mullican

whisper, Charles had women in front of the stage practically humping the legs of his piano. Even his holiday classic "Merry Christmas, Baby" (1947) exuded sexuality. Brown liked to wear matching mink capes and neckties and was compared to Little Richard, in terms of flamboyance, by their friend, singer Ruth Brown. But onstage Charles was the smooth, sexy Captain of a forlorn ship.

Originally dismissed by *Metronome* as "closely reproducing every nuance of Nat King Cole's voice and piano," Brown actually had a unique style that breaded his languid voice with a heavy gospel past. Baptist Church choir director Swannie Simpson, whose daughter Mattie gave birth to Charles at age twenty and died the day before she turned twenty-one, raised her grandson in Texas City with his grandfather, Conquest Simpson. (Coincidentally, the Simpsons were from Opelousas, Louisiana, as was the Milburn family.) After Charles got good on that church keyboard, Swannie paid for lessons for him to learn classical piano and stayed on his ass, sometimes with a switch. "His grandmother used to beat the hell out of him, but he loved her," said Caron, who listened to Brown's stories of his upbringing on the long bus rides between gigs in the '90s. He sometimes recounted detailed interactions with his mother, though she died when he was six months old.

Brown's father Mose was a ne're-do-well who drank heavily, chased women, and neglected his son. Brown told Caron that his father once left him, at age three or four, in the parlor of a cathouse while Mose went upstairs. "Charles blamed his father for his mother's death, giving her syphilis," Caron said. The 1923 death certificate of Mattie Brown lists syphilis as a contributing factor to the main cause, exhaustion from gastroenteritis (stomach flu). "Mose had moved to the Panhandle to work and he came back to Texas City to get Charles. That's when his car got stuck on the railroad tracks and he was killed by a train," Caron continued. Mose Brown died in 1928, when his son was five and a half. "Charles told me that he wondered how his life would've turned out if his father took him away from his grandparents. He said he certainly wouldn't have been a musician."

But, then, he also might not have turned into a degenerate racetrack gambler, known to drop his last $1,000 on a single race. It was Johnny Moore, sixteen years his senior, who introduced Brown to pari-mutuel wagering, an instant obsession explored in the Blazers' 1946 single "Race Track Blues." Gambling bit into Moore's business soul, so cash was always an issue between him and singer Brown, who was the star of the group no matter what the damn marquee said. When Moore sold "Drifting Blues" to Philo for $800, Brown was incensed. He wrote that song while a student at Central High in Galveston from a hymn his grandmother sang, yet had to share credit with the other two Blazers. Worse, Moore taking the short money on the future R&B Record of 1946 cost Brown hundreds of thousands of dollars he could've turned into millions at the racetrack.

Brown went solo in 1948 and hit the top five with "Get Yourself Another Fool," whose title could've been aimed at Moore. His first #1 smash was 1949's "Trouble Blues," which Sam Cooke covered in 1963 on the classic, Brown-influenced LP *Night Beat*. Lieber-Stoller's first hit "Hard Times" was Brown's last in 1952, with the title presaging the years ahead, as his records flopped, his booking agent jumped ship, and the union hounded him for dues.

"There might have been some homophobic agents or club owners," said Caron. "But the gambling hurt Charles's career more than anything. You couldn't give him any money. It would be gone in an hour."

Dropped by Aladdin in 1957, Brown and Milburn were drifting without a sail. But the duo finally caught a whiff of luck in Cincinnati in September 1960, when King Records owner Sid Nathan, also surprised that the R&B piano icons were playing some border town gambling den, sent for Brown and Milburn. "Sid Nathan said we needed to write a new Christmas song," Milburn recalled in '79. "Me and Charles were living in the same hotel room, so he went to one side to work on his song and I went to the other side to work on mine." Brown's crooner "Please Come Home For Christmas" became the seasonal radio hit (especially after the Eagles covered it in 1978), but there's nothing "B" about the flip side—

Milburn's rollicking "Christmas (Comes But Once a Year)," with its then inventive ska beat. Brown covered it on his 1961 Christmas album for King.

The pair split up, at least label-wise, when Milburn left King for Motown in 1963. In another case of bad timing, his *Return of the Blues Boss* LP was buried under the emergence of labelmates Marvin Gaye, the Supremes, and Stevie Wonder, who had their first big hits that year.

Brown and Milburn both married white women in Ohio in the mid-1960s, with Brown moving to Columbus to be with the recently widowed Eva McGhee, who "owned the largest garage in town," Brown told *Living Blues* magazine in 1994. Milburn relocated to Cleveland with third wife Ann Marie Macarol, just six years out of Euclid High. (He had earlier been married in '46 and '54.) Though the Ohio marriages didn't last, they seemed to have given some needed separation between the codependents. Brown moved to the West Coast after his divorce, playing jazzy organ in lounge trios and reconnecting with Johnny Moore, while Milburn stayed in Cleveland, where he remained a regional star.

In 1969, while playing Satan's Den in Cincinnati, Milburn's left hand stopped listening to his brain. Instead of that steady boogie-woogie bass line, there was a flail of fingers not knowing where to go. "When I went to tell the club owner, he said, 'Amos, your mouth is crooked.' I had a stroke right there onstage."

Milburn had recovered sufficiently to play a "Battle of the Blues" with Brown at a political fundraiser in 1970 at the Viking Lounge in Cincinnati. But later that year, Amos had a second stroke that left him wheelchair-bound and severely piano-challenged. Doctors ordered forty-two-year-old Milburn to quit drinking after the first stroke, but he just couldn't leave that scotch alone. "You know how stupid you can be sometimes? I went right back to 'Bad, Bad Whiskey,'" he said. "I was never a dope fiend, but I drank Canada dry."

On Milburn's final session in 1976, rerecording "One Scotch" for a West Coast R&B compilation, producer Johnny Otis had to play the left-handed parts on the piano.

While that hypnotic southpaw groove had always been a Milburn strength, Brown's trademark was a glistening right hand that played off his vocals. Johnny Moore made him practice with his left hand tied behind his back because the Blazers had a four-stringer in Eddie Williams and Brown's instinctive bass patterns were unnecessary. His left hand was relegated to foundation chords in the Blazers, but later in his career, Brown showed he could play it all, like a link between Liberace and Little Richard. "Charles was a piano savant," said Caron. "He could play anything in any key instantly, and never forgot any tunes."

A fan of Brown's vintage mellow steam, Caron had doubted aloud that the singer was still alive when he and fellow musician Michael "Hawkeye" Herman were spinning old records in Berkeley, California, one afternoon in the mid-1980s. "Charles Brown lives a couple blocks from here," Hawkeye said. An incredulous Caron found the R&B great in Section 8 housing, making extra scratch singing "Just the Way You Are" and "Bridge Over Troubled Waters" in piano lounges in the Bay Area. "He had a little spinet piano at home, but his chops were still great, his singing still great." After playing a Christmas gig with Brown, Caron convinced him to revisit his career more

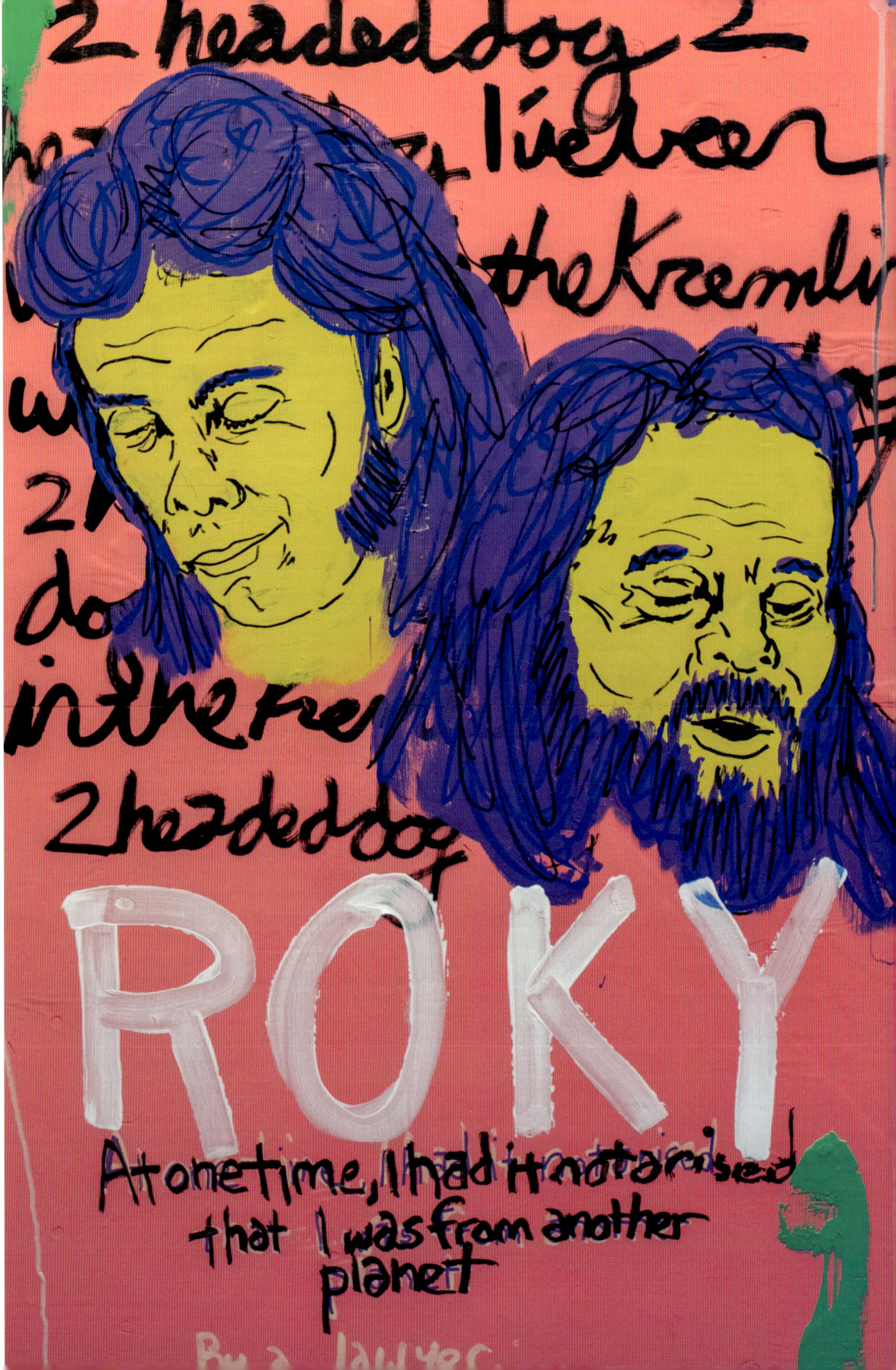
2 headed dog 2
i've been
ROKY
At one time, I had it notarised
that I was from another
planet

PART 4
Rock 'n' Rap

CHAPTER 12

Roky Erickson

Return to the River of Golden Dreams

A rafter-shaking chant of "Raw-Key! Raw-Key! Raw-Key! Raw-Key!" with an ocean of overhead hands clapping in rhythm. Walking onstage at the Hultsfred Festival in June 2007 was psychedelic rock pioneer Roky Erickson, who just six years earlier was in such a state of mental and physical dishevelment that it seemed unlikely he'd ever play another show.

But when Erickson and his band opened the Swedish set with "Cold Night for Alligators"—Erickson's voice confident and shimmering, his guitar-playing forceful and instinctive—it became sensationally apparent that this wasn't going to be a freak show but a stunning resurrection.

When the set ended a euphoric hour later with a powerful version of the 1966 cult classic "You're Gonna Miss Me," the former 13th Floor Elevators frontman reviving the banshee wail that turned Janis Joplin into a rocker, the crowd demanded an encore with such intensity that if it hadn't gotten one, there probably would have been a riot.

The comeback of Roger Kynard Erickson ("Roky," pronounced "Rocky," combines the first two letters of his first and middle names) was the most improbable in the history of rock 'n' roll, as if Syd Barrett had rejoined Pink Floyd and stolen the show.

Offstage, the man credited with inventing "acid rock" with the Elevators in the '60s was blowing minds by doing everyday things like driving a Volvo and exercising his right to vote. "It's really a miracle," said younger brother Sumner Erickson, who was awarded legal guardianship of Roky from their mother in 2001. Evelyn Erickson was an unorthodox caregiver, who supported her oldest child's decision to not take his meds, even though it meant he sometimes had to sit between walls of white noise to quiet the voices in his head. Evelyn did not want to numb her gifted child.

Roky's recovery started with medication and therapy and a move out of the section 8 housing where he lived like a hermit, except for daily visits from his mother. Sumner took him up to his home in Pittsburgh for a year, and when Roky came back down to Austin he had new teeth and a smile, though he clearly still had mental issues.

For decades, Erickson wouldn't let anyone touch him, but on recent tours of Europe and North America, he hugged fans back, signed autographs, and posed for photos after shows. But it's not like Roky could appear on a talk show. His words and thoughts don't follow usual patterns.

"Where Roky's concerned, 'normal' is just a setting on a washing machine," said tour manager Troy Campbell. "He just comes out of left field sometimes, like the other day we had pizza and I asked if he'd had enough to eat and he said 'I'm full as a ghoul.'"

"His musicianship, his voice is 100 percent back," said Clementine Hall, the queen of the acid ball when the Elevators were the house band. "But I don't know if he has the same wit and intellect. He didn't say a thing at dinner." She and ex-husband Tommy Hall, the Elevators' jug player and LSD guru, met with Roky after his San Francisco return in March 2007. The Roky she met in 1965, when Tommy poached the hellfire singer from his high school band, the Spades, and put him in front of an adventurous combo from Kerrville called the Lingsmen, was funny, unpredictable, full of offbeat energy.

Although it's assumed, because it's such a garage rock classic, that "You're Gonna Miss Me" was a hit in the summer of '66, the record peaked at #55 on the *Billboard* singles chart. It's noted more for what it inspired, plus the way it's turned into a Texas "last call" rock anthem. The debut LP *The Psychedelic Sounds of the 13th Floor Elevators* (International Artists), which includes that first single, plus "Roller Coaster," "Reverberation," and three songs from Powell St. John, was the first time "psychedelic" had been used to sell music. But this was no mere marketing ploy. This was a band that backed that far-out lifestyle all the way, with a "play the acid" mantra. They were right in time with Haight-Ashbury, though two thousand miles away.

"Tommy just wanted to get everybody high," Evelyn Erickson told me in 2007. "Well, Roky was already high. That's where the trouble started." Roky was the oldest of five boys, but was always doted on like he was the youngest. Evelyn was a former opera singer turned religious, who wrote poetry and liked to dress up. Roky's father Roger, an architect, was a workaholic and alcoholic, often away on business, so the first-born became Evelyn's neurotic obsession.

The band's habit of ingesting LSD before every performance (except drummer John Ike Walton, who swore off after a bad trip) was not conducive to a long run. Who was thinking about the future during the time of assassinations and Vietnam? The band, featuring Stacy Sutherland's proto-psych guitar, peaked with second LP *Easter Everywhere*, released eleven months after the debut. Third and final studio album *Bull of the Woods*, which finds Sutherland stepping up front for a barely there Roky, was a frazzled double LP that had its moments. But mind expansion had turned into musical excess. Without Roky's voice, the Elevators were too much like everybody else.

And that was it for the beloved cult band, which experienced a flashback of kudos after the inclusion of "You're Gonna Miss Me" (which Roky wrote as a fifteen-year-old and originally recorded with the Spades) on the landmark 1972 *Nuggets* compilation.

The band became moot when Roky pleaded insanity to avoid the penitentiary after a marijuana bust on Mount Bonnell in February 1969. But after repeated escapes from the Austin State Hospital to see his girlfriend Dana, Erickson was shipped off to the maximum security Rusk State Hospital for the criminally insane, where he spent two nightmarish years.

"The patient, a 21-year-old male, was incoherent when arrested for marijuana on Feb. 28, 1969. He has had private psychiatric care at Hedgecroft Hospital in Houston and has had electro shock treatments."—from Roky's medical report, 3/19/69, Austin State Hospital

Clementine Hall said Roky was damaged from the EST, performed without consent. "Roky escaped from Hedgecroft, and Tommy brought him to stay with me in San Francisco," she said of the summer of '68. "He was different. He said the Russians were talking to him through his teeth and that they wanted

I found my voice. I never lost it
becouse it was in Dre. Or it was in Snoop.
Or in Eazy. Or Ren.
And now it's
in these kids
in Dallas.
D
the
DOC

Curtis Mayfield's dick at the time, but I told him that name was corny as a muthafucka. [Mayfield had a hit in '73 with 'Future Shock.'] At the time, D.J. Unknown was trying to start a label called 'Def Row' and I told Dre, 'Fuck that nigga, let's call our shit Death Row,'" recalls Curry. A longtime confidant, Curry is also credited by none other than Dre for "talking me into doing this album," in the liner notes to *The Chronic*, Death Row's first release, the one that paid for all the rest.

After Griffey procured a million-dollar publishing advance from Sony Tunes Inc./Sony Songs Inc. in 1991, the new corporation that became Death Row bought recording equipment, blocked out studio time, acquired the rights for Def Row from Andre "D.J. Unknown" Manuel, and started signing artists–including Cordozar Broadus Jr., better known as Calvin Broadus and completely known as Snoop Doggy Dogg.

You can't tell it from his scratchy bray on the new sinister *Helter Skelter* LP on Giant Records, but the D.O.C. himself was once the most elastic and free-flowing rapper on the West Coast, with his 1989 debut LP, *No One Can Do It Better*, going double platinum. But just months after the record "blew up," so did Curry's follow-up dreams, as he fell asleep, drunk, behind the wheel of his car and drove off the road and into a coma.

The first concern was that Curry might not live, but after twenty-two hours of surgery, much of it reconstructive, he pulled through. The lasting injury, however, was damaged vocal chords that left him unable to speak for several months. "The only thing wrong with my voice is the way it sounds," Curry says almost six years later, "and that's getting better all the time."

No longer smooth enough to rhyme "lyrical" with "superior," Curry had to change his style to fit his excoriating voice. "I crossed over to the dark side, man, and I've seen what's coming up at the end of the millennium," Curry says. "The gangsta shit is gettin' old. You can't just get out there with a fine bitch and a blunt and a 40 [oz.] and work the crowd. That shit's been played out."

On the apocalyptic *Helter Skelter* (not-so-ironically, the working title for the proposed Dr. Dre-Ice Cube collaboration), Curry raps about rebirth, secret master plans, and the hereafter, in addition to the usual odes to "Bitchez" and his "Doggs." There's also a rhyming legal brief, titled "From Ruthless to Death Row (Do We All Part)," which summarizes Curry's past nine years: "I rose up quick from the pit/I was in 454 300 Benz/Nothin' but ends/But friends got me in a cross/Now everything's lost."

"I don't like to toot my own horn, but 'toot-toot,'" Curry says. "I'm a lyricist f'real. My job at Death Row was to make sure that all the words that came out on the albums were the shit. I'm one of the only people I know who's meticulous enough to go over every line, every word, to make sure it's all there."

Before the Dre-produced *No One Can Do It Better* hit on Eazy-E's Ruthless label, the D.O.C. made his name in his new home of Compton as a writer, with early credits including tracks on N.W.A.'s instant blacktop classic, *Straight Outta Compton* ('88), and Eazy-E's Eazy-Duz-It ('88).

"I was Eazy's pen, because he couldn't write lyrics," Curry says. "The nigga couldn't rap, either. Man, he had the worst rhythm."

Better with numbers than words, Eazy-E turned Ruthless Records—a company he claims to have started with profits from drug dealing—into the hottest label in rap. The strain of violent, sexist "gangsta rap" established the previously ignored South Central scene as the vortex of new, harder-edged hip-hop and infiltrated suburbia with tales of drive-by shootings and hooker mutilations.

At the same time, Curry insists, Eazy conducted business as if he were still on the street corner, with a focus on incoming funds and a disregard for paying out what was owed.

"In the hip-hop world, Eazy-E was the personification of evil," Curry says. "He paid my hospital bill, about $60,000, but he made me pay him back, which is cool, except that I later found out that he paid the bill out of my share of a publishing deal he made for me. The muthafucka used my money and then made me pay him back."

Curry also tells about the time he traded his publishing rights to *Straight Outta Compton*, which has sold more than five million copies and counting, for a gold necklace. "I was nineteen years old," Curry says. "I didn't know about publishing back then, and I didn't care. I was part of the hottest team in the rap game, and I just wanted to keep makin' dope records."

It was Suge Knight—whose Knightlife publishing company hit it big by owning seven tracks on Vanilla Ice's *To the Extreme* blockbuster—who convinced the D. O. C. and Dr. Dre they were being ripped off by Ruthless. When Knight exacted their release from the label—allegedly giving Eazy-E a choice between a pen in hand or a lead pipe upside the head, according to Eazy-E in Jory Farr's music-biz insider book *Moguls and Madmen*—Eazy-E and Ruthless filed a $250 million federal racketeering and extortion lawsuit against Dr. Dre, Curry, Knight, and Griffey. The suit was eventually dismissed, but Knight's reputation as "the wrong nigga to fuck with" was solidified.

"The four of us had a plan and we set it into motion," Curry says about the seeds of the partnership. "We used the money from Sony to build that company, and we did everything the right way, only I didn't get no money, but now I goin' get it." He says the last part with a singsong swagger that sounds like one of his old raps.

"I've known Suge Knight a long time. Hell, I was even tighter with him than Dre was for a while," Curry insists, "and to be totally honest with you, the dude ain't all he's cracked up to be."

Now, if Curry can only convince his mother of that.

Dr. Dre met Curry in Dallas in 1987, when Curry was a member of the Fila Fresh Crew and Dre, of World Class Wrecking Crue, was guesting on a weekly rap show hosted by Fila's Dr. Rock on KKDA-FM (K104). "Rap was just being born in Dallas, but I'd been rappin' since I was thirteen, and I was already real good at the shit," Curry says. "Dre heard me rap and, he says, 'If you come to California, nigga, we can make some money.' Me and Dre just clicked."

Curry had no qualms whatsoever about leaving a Dallas rap scene that was full of copycats. "When they first came out, Nemesis [Fila Fresh Crew's crosstown rivals] sounded like they were from Brooklyn or Queens, but then I came back two years later and they sounded like they were from Compton," Curry says. "I'm a leader, not a follower, so I moved from the projects of West Dallas to the projects of Compton."

Once in LA, where he slept on Dre's couch for the first year, Curry says he was reborn. "In Dallas, I was pretty good, but when I hit Cali I was suddenly the best. I don't know what happened, but I was un-fucking-touchable." Indeed, with *No One Can Do It Better*, the D.O.C. established himself as a raging new talent on the West Coast rap scene. Dr. Dre, who cooked up an awesome stew of live instrumentation and silky soul samples, left no question about who was rap's best producer.

"Dre is the Quincy Jones of my generation, the complete master of the studio," Curry says. "Every little sound you hear on his records, the nigga done complexed on for hours. He runs shit through his head a million times before he puts it down."

Asked if he's sad that his association with his mentor has apparently ended, Curry says, "It ain't ever over. You just go through phases of your life when you do fucked-up shit, but the real problem ain't Dre. In fact, Dre's the one who's been telling me that I needed to get a lawyer and go after my money."

"This shit ain't hidden," Curry says of his claim that he was shafted by Death Row. "Everything I've been telling you is known by those muthafuckas, but they ain't gonna say nothing because it ain't their play. This is Suge's shit, and what he says, goes."

According to the lawsuit, Interscope heads Jimmy Iovine and Ted Field, who could not be reached for comment, met privately with Knight and Dre and induced them to breach their partnership with Griffey and Curry, with Iovine calling Griffey "a crook." Dr. Dre was really the franchise, and Knight was his manager: Interscope saw no need to deal with anyone else.

"They just wrote me out," Curry says. "[Suge and Dre] have a gangsta mentality, and that's not really my mindset. Plus, I was there by myself. I didn't have no gang with me. I was lost. I didn't have no voice. I didn't know what to do, so I just rolled with the punches until I could figure out what to do."

Curry stuck it out with Death Row, overseeing and writing some lyrics for Dr. Dre's massively selling *The Chronic* LP, as well as Snoop Doggy Dogg's multiplatinum debut *Doggystyle*. "They were fuckin' with me, but I got a love for my work, and I wasn't ready to give it up," Curry says.

Whenever Curry needed money, he insists, he had to go to Knight, and "Suge wouldn't give me shit." When Curry complained and talked about getting a lawyer, he was threatened with bodily harm, according to the suit.

"They intimidated the D.O.C. right out of Los Angeles," says Joseph Porter, Curry's attorney. "He was afraid for his life. I've been threatened, too. Someone from Death Row told me that bad things happen to people who go up against them, but where does it all stop? When you do evil for a long period of time, it catches up to you, and I think we have an incredible case with stacks of documentation."

Curry says he's all the way back, and the accident that took his rapping skills and almost his life was a message from God.

"When I was in that hospital bed," he recalls, "I'd think back when I was a little kid in Dallas, and I'd pray to God: 'Please let me be the best. If you do that, I'll do right and let everybody know that it was you that put me there.' But after I got there, I reneged on my part of the deal. I was arrogant, and I thought I was invincible."

The night of the ghastly car accident, Curry says he was stopped by police in Beverly Hills and suspected of DUI. Instead of being arrested and taken to jail to sober up, however, Curry was simply given a ticket and sent on his way. Before driving off, however, he joked with the cops and took pictures of them holding his platinum record. Three hours later, Curry went through the windshield of his car and into what he calls "the edge of darkness."

"Can you believe those cops letting me go?" he says in that fucked-up voice. "Hey, maybe I should sue them." Then Curry lets out a gruff guffaw. Irony is not lost on this rapper who was deserted first by his voice, and then by his friends.

Joyce Harris
What does Color have to do with it!?

CHAPTER 14

Joyce Harris

The Rockin' Siren of Domino Records

In the summer of 1957, ten Austinites took a night school course on song marketing at the YWCA on Guadalupe Street and ended up partnering with their instructor to start a record label and music publishing company. Each pledged $5 a week to meet expenses.

These moonlighting accountants and housewives and state workers and salesmen would put out regional hits from their office above a drugstore at 607 West Twelfth Street and watch two of their acts—the Slades and Joyce Harris—lip sync on *American Bandstand*.

But by 1960, the original eleven label owners had dwindled to three. At the end of 1961, there were none.

Domino Records, Austin's first label of note, made some noise, but little money, in the years between the Elvis explosion and Beatlemania. It was an era when independent record labels flourished because, unlike the stodgy hierarchy-layered major labels, the children of Sun Records were quick to embrace rock 'n' roll as an exciting mix of black and white cultures.

Domino went even further with Joyce Harris and the Daylighters: a white singer from Louisiana backed by a black rhythm and blues band. Race was not an issue, however, because anyone who heard "No Way Out" (which critic Dave Marsh has listed as one of the greatest singles ever made) would swear the Etta James-like singer was black.

"I remember the first time we played together, thinking, 'Now this is what I'm talking about,'" said Harris, who, as a teenager, cut several singles with her younger sister Judy at Cosimo Matassa's legendary recording studio in the French Quarter. "The Daylighters took me right back to the New Orleans thing."

The band was led by Smithville native Smith, who changed his name to Sonny Rhodes, switched to lap steel guitar, and was still performing in 2019. Rounding out the group were Willie Cephas on guitar, Ira Littlefield Jr. on drums, George Underwood on bass, and Mack Moore on piano.

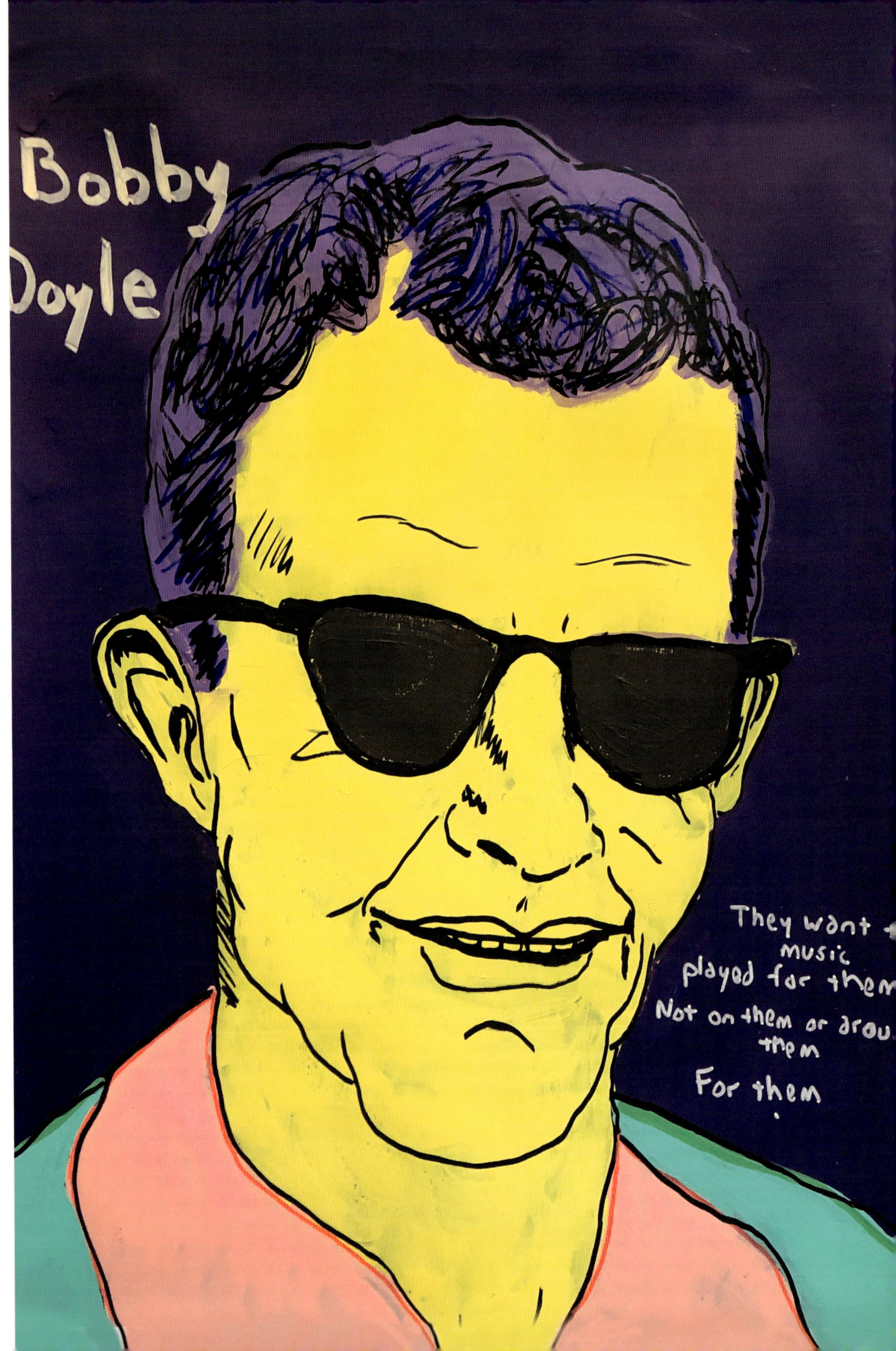
Bobby
Doyle
They want
music
played for them
Not on them or arou
them
For them

CHAPTER 15

Bobby Doyle

"Make It Beautiful"

Country superstar Kenny Rogers of Houston was a guest on *Late Night* in 1996 when David Letterman asked him who was the greatest musician he'd ever worked with. Without hesitation, Rogers answered, "Bobby Doyle."

The night that show aired, Doyle was playing a solo piano set at Ego's, a South Congress dive in the parking garage of an apartment complex. Unlike his former bass player Rogers, Doyle had to work hard for little money, playing five or six nights a week for tips and, sometimes, a small guarantee.

But if Bobby Doyle was bitter, you wouldn't know it. While the rest of the country was going "Bobby who?" this blind man in a jacket too nice for the room was wailing on a Jerry Lee Lewis number, then crooning "Fly Me to the Moon" with an extended jazz piano solo, then thumping and testifying on "Rugged Old Cross" like it was a Leon Russell number. At times he sang like country Ray Charles and then he'd channel Mose Allison on some blues that wants to be jazz that wants to be blues. It didn't matter that only a couple dozen drunks and floozies were on hand. When Bobby Doyle played, Ego's was as cool as any Greenwich Village basement club.

It doesn't happen very often, so when it does, it's something you never forget. Going into a club for no real reason and getting blown away by someone you've never heard of. It happened to me at Ego's in the '90s when I went to meet a friend who lived in the apartments. The first thing you realized about Bobby Doyle was that he knew he had IT. There's that old line about someone playing a crappy bar like it was Madison Square Garden, but in Bobby's inward eyes he was playing Carnegie Hall. A maestro's palace.

One man, one mic, one piano: nobody could do it better than Bobby Doyle. Yet, aside from a few brushes with fame—appearances in the 1960s on *The Joey Bishop Show* and *Playboy After Dark* were highlights—Doyle was a working musician with bills to pay. A man for hire who could light the fire.

"If Bobby was wearing his tuxedo and playing music for four hours, all was right in his world," said Austin pianist Nick Connolly, who met Doyle in the early '80s on the piano bar circuit. Doyle played soft enough for it to be background music, understanding that everyone in the joint was trying to get laid that night, but his romps of soul no doubt made the sex better. "They want (the music) played for them," Doyle told an interviewer in 2005. "Not on them or around them. For them."

Austin is a town full of musicians who never quite make it big as their talent, but nobody was more overloaded with gifts than Doyle, who was a rock 'n' roll piano prodigy busting out of McCallum High in the late '50s, played the jazz cocktail circuit nationwide, and sang for Columbia Records in the '60s. Doyle replaced David Clayton Thomas in Blood, Sweat & Tears for a minute in 1972, and then spent the last three decades of his career in the piano bars of Austin.

To the mainstream he'll remain a footnote—the man who showed Kenny Rogers the way to a musical career. But to those of us lucky enough to sit so close to that musical force, Bobby Doyle left a lasting impression as a solo artist as intense as any five-piece band. He understood how to communicate a song. The rest is noise.

A heavy smoker, as were most of his fans, Doyle succumbed to lung cancer on July 30, 2006, at age sixty-six. Folks that knew him well, like Threadgill's owner Eddie Wilson, a former McCallum High classmate, said Doyle "was ready to go the day after (wife) Mary died" two years earlier. Mary Cockrill Doyle, whom he wed in 1988, was much more than her husband's eyes, providing vocal support near his side at every show. Their interplay made every gig fun.

After putting Ego's on the map in the mid-1990s, it turned into something else, a rock club, and Doyle left for gigs at Eddie V's and the Driskill. His kind of places with his kind of people. He kept playing until he got the diagnosis that his cancer was terminal, and he became too weak. In March 2006, about five months before his death, Doyle set up a couple mics at his home in North Austin and invited his former musical partner Joyce Webb, whom he met in the '50s, to lay down some tracks. He was known as a song interpreter, not a writer, but his composition "Beautiful," recorded when he was too frail to play gigs, is hauntingly gorgeous. I played it over and over again, that tune about finding a balance between the loneliness that creativity requires and the need for human love. At least that's the way I heard it.

Thanks to ninety-one-year-old Fleetwood Richards of Onion Creek, whose association with Doyle goes back to Houston in the early '70s, I was able to copy several Doyle CDs that were never in print, as well as the terrific 1996 studio recording with engineer Spencer Starnes that Mary Doyle sold at gigs. My favorite of the seven CDs is probably "Live From the Roulette Club Houston 1973," which features Doyle and Webb trading lead vocals for the first hour, then the whole quartet—including drummer Steve Kellar and bassist Bob Buelow—singing four-part harmonies on "Their Hearts Were Full of Spring" to close it out. This cover of the 1960 song by the Four Freshmen was the first song played at Doyle's funeral—at the angels' request.

I knew Bobby Doyle as a piano man, a lounge lizard, a soul belter. "Spring" told me I didn't know Doyle at all, so I went searching into details from his life that might piece together some kind of a story. The Austin great was never the subject of a major feature.

He was born in Houston on August 14, 1939, to Edward and Ella Doyle, a carpenter and a housewife. Robert Glen, the youngest of six children, was born blind, an affliction attributed to his mother contracting German measles while pregnant with him. When Bobby reached school age, the Doyles moved to Austin so he could attend the School for the Blind and Visually Impaired on West Forty-Fifth Street.

Bobby wanted to be like the other kids, so he opted to attend high school at McCallum High, becoming the first blind graduate in 1958. The next year, a school organization that had raised $1,700 for a bus trip to Mexico instead donated the money to Doyle for a surgery that might restore his eyesight.

It didn't, and Doyle had to be content with

THE BOBBY DOYLE TRIO

having what Austin bassist Jon Blondell said were "the ears of a bat." Eddie Wilson recalled Doyle with a transistor radio in his pocket in class, listening to his beloved baseball at a volume level the teacher couldn't hear.

Doyle lettered in wrestling at McCallum, and also tried out for the team at University of Texas, which he attended from 1958 to 1960 before dropping out to play music full time. "He told me once, 'never let a blind man get his hands on you, because he'll never let you go,'" recalls his old pal Fleetwood. "He was a wiry Irishman, not to be messed with."

Kenny Rogers (left in the above photo) remembered, in his recent *Luck Or Something Like It* autobiography, that Doyle struggled with alcohol and once was so soused at a gig in Houston that he snubbed the great Tony Bennett, who had asked if he could sing a couple with the band. "In a minute, Tony," Doyle said, going in to his next number while Rogers and drummer Don Russell shook their heads in apology. "But even at his worst," Rogers wrote of a lit-up Doyle, "he was better than anyone else I'd ever heard."

By the time Doyle formed his trio with Rogers in 1960, he'd already gone a few rounds with rock 'n' roll. As a senior at McCallum and a member of the school's Talent, Incorporated club, Doyle played a fifteen-minute set of rock and doo-wop on KVET-AM every Saturday.

Doyle's single on the Domain label, "Here Now," went nowhere, and he followed his family back to Houston. There he came to the attention of notorious Duke/Peacock label owner Don Robey, who had started the Back Beat label to cash in on the rock 'n' roll craze. Robey's offshoot eventually hit paydirt with "Treat Her Right" by Roy Head and the Traits hitting #2 nationally, but Doyle was dropped after two singles on the label: "Pauline" b/w "Someone Else, Not Me" (9/59) and "Hot Seat" b/w "Unloved" (3/60).

Doyle used to sometimes compare his diverse musical interests to living in a house with many rooms, so you could say he spent the '60s walking the hall between rock/doo-wop and vocal jazz. Doyle found Rogers, a struggling singer, in Houston and turned him into a bassist/high harmony singer in the Bobby Doyle Three. Drummer Russell sang as well on 1962's *In a Most Unusual Way* (Columbia),

which sounds almost psychedelic today for its over-the-top vocal arrangements.

It was a style that didn't catch on with the mainstream, though the trio became popular on the cocktail jazz circuit across the country. When they played the Melody Room on Sunset Strip, better known today as the Viper Room, a young actor and piano fanatic named Clint Eastwood was in the audience every night. Before he was known as Dr. John, LA session player Mac Rebennack was another Doyle fan. The public had no idea who Bobby Doyle was, but the musicians knew.

"How could you be a player and watch Bobby and not be impressed?" wondered Connolly. "He could play every kind of music imaginable for four hours and it was all in his head."

After Rogers and Russell left to play in the more popular Kirby Stone Four, still riding that 1958 hit "Baubles, Bangles and Beads," Doyle reconfigured the trio with Webb sharing leads. The new Bobby Doyle Three got a regular gig at a private club in LA called the Factory, where all the movie stars and other celebs went so they wouldn't be mobbed. It was the Rat Pack's West Coast haunt, and one night an impressed Sammy Davis Jr. offered an opening gig in Las Vegas.

Connolly said he was watching a documentary about 1960s Las Vegas recently when something in a tiny corner of the screen caught him. "They had a 1959 Cadillac convertible with a tripod in the back panning the marquees," he said. "I rewinded a few seconds and paused it. Yep, right there, in a row, were the names 'Frank Sinatra,' 'Buddy Hackett,' and 'The Bobby Doyle Three.'"

Doyle was a regular on the Strip and in nearby Lake Tahoe until he, first wife Sammie Lou (a Beaumont native he married in 1961), and their four young children moved back to Austin in the mid-1970s. He got a gig four nights a week playing a Vegas-themed club named Caesar's, which had recently opened at 1907 East Riverside. After that club closed around 1978, Doyle worked regularly at such joints as the North Forty, the Cloak Room, the Blue Parrot, and the Ramada Inn on East Eleventh. He was a journeyman with eighty eight keys in his toolbox.

Sadly, Doyle's records are all out of print, including 1970's *Nine Songs* on Bell Records, with Steve Cropper on guitar. Recorded at Sun Studios in Memphis, Doyle called *Nine Songs* a favorite of his records, but the Bobby Doyle Three was "the best band I've ever played in." Bobby, Kenny, and Don worked their tails off for five years.

Hopefully, someone will put together a proper Bobby Doyle reissue. A career retrospective for a guy who never had a hit and played out-of-fashion music for lonely people in dark rooms. But the musicians knew. Bobby Doyle was always a star among players. When Kenny Rogers flew Bobby to Los Angeles for a fiftieth birthday show in 1988, producer Quincy Jones was the first to his feet after Doyle's segment, leading a rousing standing ovation.

To have that much of a gift and never make it big is better than having only marginal talent and selling a million copies. That's the true artist creed and Bobby Doyle lived it to the very end.

Sonny Curtis
One thing that did have an early influence on me was Mexican music

CHAPTER 16

Sonny Curtis

Who Can Turn the World on with a Song?

West Texan Sonny Curtis could very well be the Bo Jackson of songwriting. Instead of excelling in two sports, the Meadow product penned two classics that are as different as football and baseball.

As a Slaton sandstorm howled outside his window in the summer of 1958, he wrote "I Fought the Law," one of the original rock rebellion songs. First recorded by the Crickets three months after Buddy Holly died, "I Fought" was made famous by the Bobby Fuller Four in 1965, then flagged as a nascent punk song by the Clash. The other landmark composition came in 1970 after Curtis received a four-page synopsis of a TV show about a thirty-year-old woman out on her own after an engagement breakup. In a couple hours he came up with "Love Is All Around," better known today as the theme to *The Mary Tyler Moore Show*.

The garage rock holy grail and a Minneapolis anthem that came to represent feminism with a thrown beret in the air. Two songs that had nothing in common except they came from the creative mind of Sonny Curtis, born in a dugout his daddy built on a farm thirty miles outside of Lubbock during the Great Depression.

Curtis also had hits with "Walk Right Back" for the Everly Brothers, "Someday" by Webb Pierce, "The Straight Life" for Bobby Goldsboro, "Destiny's Child" by Waylon Jennings, "I'm No Stranger to the Rain" for Keith Whitley, and "More Than I Could Say" (with Jerry Allison) by Bobby Vee and, later, Leo Sayer.

But even if he didn't write a single song, Curtis would be a notable figure in rock 'n' roll history for his close association with Holly, less than a year older, whom Curtis played guitar and fiddle with before Buddy formed the Crickets. Curtis was in the band—along with Jerry Allison on drums and Don Guess on bass—when Buddy Holly opened for Elvis Presley at Lubbock's Fair Park Coliseum in April 1956. "We had become Elvis clones overnight," Curtis told *Songwriter* magazine.

Before that, Buddy, Sonny, and Bob Montgomery played country on DDAV's "Sunday Party" radio show. Curtis grew up around the bluegrass played by his uncles, the Mayfield Brothers, whose leader Edd replaced guitarist Carter Stanley in Bill Monroe's band in 1951. By the time he met Holly at age fifteen, Sonny was known as one of the hottest pickers in Lubbock and played the first Fender Stratocaster in the area. "I admired Sonny Curtis so much I wanted to change my name to Sonny," Waylon Jennings once told an interviewer. "I even wanted to stand like him." Holly, Curtis, and Guess formed a band they called Buddy and the Two Tones, which recorded for Decca in Nashville in early 1956.

Not much came of the sojourns to Bradley's Barn—two rockabilly singles ("Blue Days, Black Nights," "Modern Don Juan") went nowhere—but Curtis got his first cut as a writer when Holly recorded "Rock Around With Ollie Vee." Curtis got the name from the wife of a black farmhand who worked for his dad and lived at the farm.

Curtis said he practically forced himself to become a songwriter a year earlier, after a gig opening for Hank Snow in Lubbock. "I was so naïve I thought that if I covered Hank Snow's hits, he'd be flattered and the audience would love it," Curtis said of a set list that included "I'm Movin' On." Instead, Curtis was met with the wrath of Snow's road manager. "He told me to write my own damn hit songs," Curtis recalled. He was a guitar player who hadn't really considered that possibility before.

Buddy Holly decided he wanted to play lead guitar, with Curtis switching to rhythm, at around the time Slim Whitman was looking for a touring guitarist, so a wounded Curtis took the gig and left Lubbock. In '57, he hooked up with the Phillip Morris Roadshow, backing Carl Smith, Goldie Hill, Red Sovine, and others in the package tour. He took whatever gig he could, and when "That'll Be the Day," "Peggy Sue," and "Oh Boy" hit in quick succession for Buddy and the Crickets, Curtis was playing five sets a night at a Colorado ski lodge. "The pay wasn't very good," Curtis has said of that gig, "but the hours were long."

When Holly moved to NYC in '58, the Crickets decided to stay in Lubbock "because there was no place to ride their motorcycles in New York," said Curtis, who started playing again with Allison and bassist Joe B. Mauldin. They were working on new material when Buddy died in a plane crash in February 1959 at age twenty-two. "He was so far ahead of the curve, who knows how far Buddy would've gone?" said his former guitar player.

The Crickets were driving to New York in 1960 to work on *In Style with the Crickets*, their first album without Holly, when Curtis played them "I Fought the Law" from the backseat. It was closer to country at first, but Allison took care of that, with one of the great propulsive drum beats on record. Amarillo's Earl Sinks sang in the studio sessions, but a guitarist/singer in El Paso named Bobby Fuller would soon make the song his own.

After a tremendous 1960 British tour with the Crickets backing the Everly Brothers, Curtis got a draft notice and had to leave the group. But he's been a Cricket since returning from two years in the service in 1962.

After the army, Curtis settled in Los Angeles, where there was songwriting and guitar playing work. He paid the bills writing and singing jingles ("You Deserve a Break Today" for McDonald's) but also occasionally played guitar for Roger Miller, who shared management with Mary Tyler Moore. Curtis said he'd give it a try when he was asked to write a song for the intro of *The Mary Tyler Moore Show* and later that afternoon found himself in the office of show creator James L. Brooks. "We're not ready to choose a theme song," Brooks said, but after Curtis played him "Love Is All Around," a tape recorder materialized and the pitch process was over. "Let me take that song with me to Minneapolis," Brooks told Curtis. The music came before the intro footage.

Not many folks know that the lyrics were altered after the first season. The unforgettable first line, "Who can turn the world on with her smile?" was not in the original version. When the show debuted, the Mary Richards character had embarked on a fresh start, but didn't have a job or, really, any skills or experience to be more than a secretary. The theme song's original first line was "How will you make it on your own?"

Applying for an entry-level job, Richards

was instead hired on Lou Grant's whim as assistant producer of the "Six O'Clock News," so by the end of the season a more optimistic tone was needed for the theme. Besides the new opener, the last line was changed from "You just might make it after all," to "You're gonna make it after all."

Curtis had hoped that he'd also sing the theme song, but the show's producers wanted to find a "name" vocalist. "They were going for Andy Williams, who was hotter'n a pistol and had his own show," recalled Curtis. "So I said, 'Well, if you can get Andy Williams, then go ahead." When Williams passed, Curtis got the gig—and a Top 30 country hit. The song has also been covered by rockers Joan Jett and Husker Du, in homage to their home town of Minneapolis.

One of his later compositions to get attention was "The Real Buddy Holly Story," which inspired Holly fanatic Paul McCartney to make a documentary of the same name to dispel some of the mistruths of the 1978 film starring Gary Busey.

"It was a good Hollywood rock and roll movie," said Curtis, "but it didn't capture Buddy to my way of thinking." The scene that especially irked Curtis was when Holly, frustrated by the meddling of Nashville producer Owen Bradley, punches him out in the studio. "I was there," said Curtis, "and nothing like that ever happened. It was always, 'yes, sir, Mr. Bradley' or 'no, sir.' Buddy always treated everyone with respect."

Sonny Curtis said when Buddy and the Crickets hit, it was like watching a train going somewhere special—and you're not on it. But destined for greatness, he got there a different way and must be considered up there with the greatest Texas songwriters ever.

Jimmy Bowen
The worst mistake
a producer can make is to
think it's his album. A good producer should
do as little as possible- or as much as
necessary.

PART 5

Moguls and Mentors

CHAPTER 17

Jimmy Bowen

New Sheriff in Town

The twenty-five-year-old Texan sat in the limo outside a Palm Springs desert compound for about an hour, waiting for Frank Sinatra. The junior exec had been recently hired by Reprise Records, which had half a dozen strong acts, but the problem was that there were over a hundred on the label. Reprise was founded by Sinatra in 1960 and rescued by parent company Warner Brothers, with Sinatra retaining one-third ownership, three years later. That's when Jimmy Bowen came aboard. "Sinatra would have a few drinks in some lounge and sign the piano player. He was out of control," recalled Bowen, the sheriff's son from the Texas Panhandle. "So one of my first jobs was to tell Mr. Sinatra we had to drop more than half the acts he'd signed. I was scared shitless, knowing he was going to fire me—or worse." Finally called inside, Bowen laid out the direness of the situation. "Sinatra gulped a glass of Jack Daniels, and then he said, 'Well, do what you gotta do,' and walked away. I left before he could change his mind." The long ride to Palm Springs was a lot shorter on the way back.

When Bowen told the story thirty years later, he was Music City's feared "Chairman of the Board." When your music biz baptism was firing about seventy friends of Frank Sinatra, it's no big deal to clean house when you take over as head of a Nashville label, which Bowen did six times from 1976 to his 1995 retirement. As the incoming chief at MGM, MCA (twice), Elektra/Asylum, Warner Brothers, and Capitol, he'd generally keep two or three people and fire the rest. Bowen even pink-slipped the A&R guy who signed Garth Brooks, Capitol's golden goose in a Stetson. The designated label-fixer axed so many people he stopped going to industry parties. "The last one that I went to, I looked around the room and realized that I had fired half the people there—some of them two or three times," Bowen said.

In a town known for humility, where honchos ask if you'd like some coffee, then fetch it themselves, Bowen made sure everyone knew who was boss. "Whenever you have a meeting with Bowen, you have to go to him," said MCA's Tony Brown, then Bowen's main rival. Wearing a Greek sailor cap and aviator glasses, Bowen brought the Rat Pack mentality to the Hat Act reality and never really fit in.

"I was a Yankee for the first time in my life," Bowen said of his two decades running (some might say "ruining") Nashville.

But here's where Jimmy Bowen really matters: he produced sixty-seven #1 country singles and ten #1 country albums in the '70s and '80s, making superstars out of Kenny Rogers, Hank Williams Jr., Reba McEntire, Conway Twitty, and George Strait. "The music belongs to the artist," was his credo, something else he said he learned from Sinatra. "The worst mistake a producer can make is to think it's his record. A good producer should do as little as possible—or as much as necessary."

Bowen arrived in Nashville with a proven track record in the pop field, producing signature songs for Sinatra ("Strangers in the Night"), Dean Martin ("Everybody Loves Somebody"), and Sammy Davis Jr. ("I've Gotta Be Me"), with arranger/conductor Ernie Freeman.

He started getting a little cocky after winning 1967's Record of the Year Grammy for "Strangers in the Night," but Sinatra was still in charge of the recording sessions. "He'd usually nail it on the first take, but sometimes there'd be a second take," recalled Bowen. "But that was it. Frank didn't do a third." After Sinatra's second take of "That's Life," Bowen said, "Let's try one more," and Sinatra shot back "No, we got it!" But Bowen persisted, and Sinatra called him a "fuckin' hayseed!" in front of everybody (including fiancée Mia Farrow), and stormed out. But about ten minutes later, Sinatra was back. "ONE MORE TAKE!" he said, and that was the one they used on the classic "That's Life." That's why he's practically spitting the lyrics in his most over-the-top performance.

Bowen famously butted heads with Garth Brooks in the early '90s, but as a label exec, not a producer. Although Bowen oversaw multimillion sellers *No Fences* in 1990 and *Ropin' the Wind* in '91, Brooks blamed Bowen for slower sales of *The Chase* in 1992 and *In Pieces* in 1993. And why the hell did he have to change the label's name from Capitol Nashville (AKA "The House That Garth Built") to Liberty and move the offices miles away from Music Row? Brooks wanted a deal like the one Michael Jackson had signed, giving him more than a 25 percent royalty rate; Bowen told him he wasn't Michael Jackson, which, according to Bowen's 1997 *Rough Mix* autobiography, pissed off Brooks to no end. In 1994, Brooks told honchos at Capitol's parent company EMI that he wouldn't deliver his next album if Bowen was still in charge.

The pay-per-view-worthy stare down between the control freaks was averted, however, when the label head was diagnosed with thyroid cancer in late 1994 and retired to Maui. Bowen, who must've gotten a good chuckle with Garth's *Life of Chris Gaines* debacle in '99, was living in Arizona with fifth wife Ginger in early 2019. Liberty was changed back to Capitol Nashville after Bowen left, and the offices returned to Music Row.

Thousand Dollar Money Order

"I didn't really like country music growing up," said the Dumas native, who teamed with fellow West Texas State student Buddy Knox in 1956 to chase the Elvis vapors to the top of the charts.

They called their rockabilly band the Orchids and wore matching purple shirts. After Roy Orbison of Wink and his Teen Kings played the college in Canyon, Bowen asked him where he got that great sound on "Ooby Dooby," his first single. "Norman Petty's studio in Clovis," Orbison said.

A few weeks later, bassist Bowen and guitarists Knox and Don Lanier, with session drummer Dave Alldred, crossed the border into New Mexico to see if they had some magic in their music. They paid Petty $300 for the April '56 all-day session and left with the masters, a policy that Petty would change with Buddy Holly, who started making records at Petty's in 1957. The resulting self-released single—"Party Doll" by Buddy Knox with the Orchids b/w "I'm Stickin' With You" by Jimmy Bowen with the Orchids—attracted the attention of NYC's Roulette Records (Lanier's sister was a model in New York and knew co-owners Morris Levy and Phil Kahl). "He had a real Mafia voice," Bowen said of Levy's phone call. "'Hey kid, I like your rekkid. I'm gonna send you some money to come to New York.'" When

the money order for a thousand dollars came the next day, it took Bowen all day to cash it. "It was probably the biggest money order in Dumas up to that time."

Roulette split the regional single into two 45s—with B-sides by Knox and Bowen recorded in New York City—and renamed the band Rhythm Orchids. "Party Doll" was Roulette's first #1 record, while Bowen's single, with "Everlovin' Fingers" on the flip side, hit #14. Bowen released several more 45s on Roulette, but none hit the Top 40. "When the girls stopped screaming and I could hear myself sing," Bowen said in '93, "I figured I needed to find another way into the music business." The real-life model for the Hesh character in *The Sopranos*, Levy gave the kids from Texas a glimpse into the real-life music business, where payola ran radio and a couple thugs materialized whenever the subject of monies owed came up. "You want royalties," Levy would bellow, "then go to England!"

Bowen laughed at the memory of the first label exec he met, who may have instilled a little gangster mentality. We were sitting in a whatever room in Bowen's brick mansion on Franklin Road in late '93. He rarely went into the Liberty office, he said, because that's where they think about the present. "My mind is on next September," he said. But not on this day, when Bowen seemed to enjoy reminiscing for a career profile in the *Dallas Morning News*.

After a brief time doing A&R for Bob Marcucci's Chancellor Records (Frankie Avalon, Fabian), Bowen was hired as a staff producer at Reprise in 1963. One of his first projects with the label was "The Lonely Surfer" by Jack Nitzsche, which reached #39 on the charts. But it was his work on *The Intimate Keely Smith* and Dean Martin's "Everybody Loves Somebody," which knocked the Beatles out of #1 in 1964, that put producer Bowen on Sinatra's radar like a jumbo jet. Ol' Blue Eyes had recorded "Everybody Loves Somebody" seventeen years earlier, and it went nowhere. Rising star Bowen became part of the inner circle when he married Keely Smith, a close friend of Sinatra's, in '65. He also helped first daughter Nancy Sinatra by putting her with Lee Hazlewood of Port Neches, who cowrote and produced smash hit "These Boots Are Made for Walking" in 1966. When the Sinatra father/daughter duet had a #1 hit the next year with "Something Stupid," Bowen was listed as coproducer, though he wasn't in the studio. The kid from West Texas was learning how the music business worked.

Bowen and Louis Prima's ex had a messy divorce in 1969, by which time Bowen had formed AMOS Records (Artists Music and Other Stuff) as a mirror of Reprise, signing such past-prime acts as Bing Crosby, Frankie Laine, Mel Carter, and Johnny Tillotson, but also as a launching pad for new talent. The label didn't have a single hit record in its three years, but two AMOS acts would play a part in music history, when Glenn Frey of Longbranch Pennywhistle and Don Henley of Shiloh joined together with Bernie Leadon and Randy Meisner to form the Eagles. AMOS LPs by Longbranch and Shiloh (whose membership also included J. D. Souther and future Warner Brothers Nashville president Jim Ed Norman, respectively) stiffed, but the collaborative offshoot released two of the three best-selling albums of all time, with *Their Greatest Hits 1971-1975* and *Hotel California* sandwiching Michael Jackson's *Thriller*.

Bowen's country music mentor was Tompall Glaser, whose Hillbilly Central recording studio in Nashville helped birth the '70s "country outlaw" movement with recordings by Waylon Jennings, Billy Joe Shaver, Mickey Newbury, Kris Kristofferson, and many more. When he moved to Nashville in '76, Bowen hung out at sessions and listened to every classic country record Glaser thought he should hear. He also quit drinking Jack and started smoking weed instead. Bowen's apprenticeship was officially over when he encouraged Hank Williams Jr. to pursue his true identity as a rowdy country rocker. "Family Tradition" was a Bowen production.

Texas can boast several top record producers as native sons. T Bone Burnett of Fort Worth helmed the multi-platinum *O Brother Where Art Thou?* soundtrack (2001) and *Raising Sand* by Alison Krauss and Robert Plant (2007), in addition to acclaimed LPs by Los Lobos (*How Will the Wolf Survive?*), Gillian Welch *(Revival)*, and Elvis Costello (*King of America*). Jim Beck of Dallas helped create the honky-tonk sound with recordings by Lefty Frizzell, Ray Price, Marty Robbins, and many others in the early '50s, before he died after accidentally inhaling cleaning solution. Houston's Huey Meaux, the barber with the golden ear, produced classic garage rock by Sir Douglas Quintet, R&B by Barbara Lynn, and country by Freddy Fender.

Then there were Tom Wilson of Waco and Hillsboro's Bob Johnston, who produced not only classic '60s Bob Dylan albums (Johnston took over for Wilson on *Highway 61 Revisited*), but the Velvet Underground, the Animals, Frank Zappa, and Sun Ra (Wilson) and Johnny Cash, Leonard Cohen, and Simon & Garfunkel (Johnston) as well. Amazing bodies of work from two guys who grew up forty miles from each other in the middle of Texas.

But no one's resume is more impressive than Bowen's. Before he was thirty, he produced classic recordings by Frank Sinatra and Dean Martin. Then came all those number ones in Nashville. Bowen also spearheaded Nashville's conversion to digital recording technology in 1986—a year before Los Angeles studios followed suit.

The knock on Bowen, who produced an average of one album a month for fifteen years, was that he was just in the room—when he wasn't on the golf course. He usually shared production credit with the artist, but that's how Bowen wanted it, to get the full commitment of the person whose music this was. When Reba, then a moderately successful country pop singer, signed to MCA in 1984, she told label boss Bowen she wanted to go back to her roots, with fiddles and steel guitar. He gave her the keys to make *My Kind of Country*, and McEntire won her first of four consecutive CMA awards for best female vocalist. There are a lot of stories like that.

Many of those Bowen fired became label heads and other prominent Nashvillians, which could be why his name is not suitably revered today. But nobody mastered both the business and creative sides, in both the pop and country fields, like Jimmy Bowen. He did it his way. Who cares how many people show up for his funeral?

The last album he produced, '94's *Healing Hands of Time* by Willie Nelson, took him back to the Reprise years with its lush wash of strings bathing both pop standards and country classics penned by Willie. Working with a live orchestra in the studio again, Jimmy Bowen had come full circle on a career that made enemies but also a lot of money. There are a lot of folks in Nashville mansions who love Jimmy Bowen.

But it was the music that turned him on the most. Okay, maybe the power, too, and the knowledge that comes through experience. Bowen said he operated under a simple mantra: "You make music for tomorrow, not for today," which as a former one-hit-wonder he understands better than most. Nashville started standing still in the '90s, he said, because radio became everything. "There are too many people making music on purpose," he said, preferring when artists wrote songs because they had something to say, not to emulate #1 hits. Trends and friends come and go, but a great record is eternal.

CHAPTER 18

B. L. Joyce, Kenny Dorham, and Gil Askey

"Extensions of Him"

Trumpet players blew so hard to produce the slightest spit of sound that they almost passed out. Drummers snapped their sticks with all the rhythmic sense of a pair of tennis shoes in the dryer. The honks of confusion rang out in the music room on the first day of band practice.

It was 1950, and Austin native Alvin Patterson, a twenty-seven-year-old recent graduate of the New England Conservatory of Music, sat in his office at Douglass High School in El Paso and wondered what he'd gotten himself into. The school had never had a band before. His thoughts turned to his mentor, B. L. Joyce, the larger-than-life band director at L. C. Anderson High School in East Austin from 1933–1955.

Patterson wondered how the man he called "Prof" would handle the situation. He took a deep breath, thrust open the door of his office, and stood firmly before his musical beginners, but the dissonance barely dispersed.

THWACK! Patterson brought his baton down hard and the room froze. "Rule number one," Patterson intoned. "When I step up to the podium I want to be able to hear a pin drop."

Patterson sat in his home office/Anderson High museum in East Austin and smiled at the memory. "I always thought Mr. Joyce was maybe a little too strict until I had to control a room full of kids with noisemakers in their hands," said the eighty-one-year-old recent retiree. "You've gotta demand discipline and respect or there's gonna be chaos."

The Anderson High School Yellow Jacket Band, whose lofty alumni include bop trumpet great Kenny Dorham and former Motown arranger and band leader Gil Askey, had only two directors in its thirty-eight-year history. Patterson took over in 1955, when Joyce was forced to resign because of a new statewide regulation that required high school band directors to have music degrees. That Joyce, who got his college degree in tailoring from Tuskegee Institute in Alabama, didn't step down voluntarily made for a rough return for Patterson.

"If there was anybody you could call a legend in East Austin during that time, it was B. L. Joyce," said Joseph Reid, who played clarinet in Joyce's last and Patterson's first bands. It was like taking over for Bear Bryant at Alabama, but it helped that Patterson was a star player for the coach. The 1940 Anderson grad was eventually able to carve his own imposing legacy at Anderson until 1971, when Austin's historically black high school was closed and its students bused to predominantly white schools.

Long before Janis Joplin sang at Threadgill's and Willie Nelson got the heads and necks together at the Armadillo, Austin's reputation as a music town was forged by the Anderson High School band. Resplendent in uniforms as bright as a September sunrise, the Yellow Jacket Band would trek to the annual Prairie View Interscholastic League competitions and usually come back with a trophy. Under Joyce's directorship, the Jacket band won the state championship seven times from 1940 to 1953.

"If we got second place it was a big disappointment," said Ernie Mae Miller, a tenor sax player with the band from 1940 to 1943, who went on to a lengthy career as a singer/pianist. "We just sounded better than the other bands. When they called our name as the winner, we were like, 'Of course!'"

For most of the '40s, '50s, and '60s, the East Side was invisible to the rest of Austin. The black neighborhood on the other side of the freeway might as well have been a town far away. But when the Yellow Jacket Band marched down Congress Avenue to the State Capitol in 1959 for Governor John Connally's inauguration, they made all of Austin proud.

Benjamin Leo Joyce played tuba in the army band during World War I. With a desire to give black students the same kind of musical training given in the white schools, the master tailor, who taught the trade at Samuel Huston College, started canvassing East Austin in late 1932 looking for kids who wanted to play. He also solicited neglected instruments.

Joyce made the uniforms that first year; no beginning band ever looked so snappy. The players were expected to carry themselves in a manner consistent with their sartorial splendor. "Mr. Joyce didn't put up with an ounce of foolishness," said Ernie Mae, whose grandfather Laurine Cecil Anderson was the school's namesake. "You couldn't play no jazz neither."

Joyce bent his strict "no jazz" rule only one time that Patterson could remember. "We were playing football against Wheatley (the archrival from San Antonio) and they were beatin' us," he recalled. "But even worse, their band was showing us up, playing all these hot big band swing numbers. So Mr. Joyce called me over and said, 'What was that swing thing you were playing the other day when you thought I was out of listening range?' I said that was 'Tuxedo Junction' and he said, 'Okay, let's hear it.'" As Dorham played the Erskine Hawkins part perfectly, even Joyce had a smile on his face. The Anderson football team rallied to win the game.

Kenny Dorham and the Poetry of Jazz

Though Dorham went on to iconic status, replacing Miles Davis in the Charlie Parker Quintet in 1948 and cofounding the influential Jazz Messengers in '54, he often deferred to the older players in backyard jam sessions, especially Hermie Edwards, recognized as the baddest horn player in East Austin at the time. "Kenny was quiet, deep," Patterson recalled. "Very thoughtful and perceptive."

Austin is, historically, a country and blues burg, a rock-without-borders haven, a place that embraces songwriters who can make poetry from their past. You don't hear much about Austin's legacy as a jazz town, but a pair of Austinites—trumpeter Dorham and bassist Gene Ramey—played on many of the late '40s and early '50s Thelonious Monk sessions one critic called "among the most significant and original in modern jazz." To go from L. C. Anderson High School in East Austin to Fif-

ty-Second Street in Manhattan and play with the best is a trek that only talent can guide. But Dorham and Ramey, who both picked up a lot of session work by knowing how to best shade the outline of the spotlight, are not widely known except to jazz aficionados. Dorham was in the shadow of Miles Davis and Dizzy Gillespie, but he'd settle for the "thinking man's trumpet player."

After high school, Dorham attended Wiley College in Marshall, where he majored in chemistry. But after only a year, Dorham was drafted into the army. He was discharged in 1943.

Dorham's first trumpet gig was in California with the Russell Jacquet Orchestra, according to Dave Oliphant's *Texan Jazz* (University of Texas Press). Dorham got his big break in 1945 when he replaced Fats Navarro in Billy Eckstine's orchestra, the first bop big band, from whose ranks flowed Parker, Miles, Dizzy, and Dexter Gordon.

On Christmas Eve 1948, Miles Davis couldn't make a gig with the Charlie Parker Quintet, so he recommended Dorham as a replacement. The gig lasted two years, including a sensational stint in 1949 in Paris, at that city's first international jazz festival. When you play next to Bird every night, you want to be on what he's on, to hell with health.

Although Dorham was onstage with Parker on the sax great's final public performance in 1955, he spent most of the early '50s freelancing for Monk, Bud Powell, Sonny Stitt, and others. He shot dope and blew dark tone poems.

Replaced by Donald Byrd, Dorham left Art Blakey and the Jazz Messengers after only a year to form his own group, recording such lauded albums as *Afro Cuban* in 1955, *Jazz Contrasts* in '57, and his most highly regarded LP, 1963's *Una Mas*, which began his association with young sax player Joe Henderson and featured a young Tony Williams on drums. Because he wasn't flashy like Diz or as stylish as Miles, Dorham's profile stayed low, but fellow players marveled at the lyricism of his articulations. No one played with more tenderness and vulnerability.

Dorham returned home, with fellow native Austinite Teddy Wilson and an all-star cast, including John Coltrane, Elvin Jones, Lightnin' Hopkins, and Dave Brubeck, to play the 1966 Longhorn Jazz Fest at the old Disch Field (next to City Coliseum). "Kenny was so happy to see everybody and we were so happy to see him," recalled Patterson. But six years later, Dorham was dead of kidney failure at age forty-eight.

Motown's Glue, Gil Askey

Gilbert Askey may have been the second-greatest trumpet player to come out of the Yellow Jackets Band, but he was the only one to garner an Oscar nomination—for his *Lady Sings the Blues* score.

"I left Austin for good at age seventeen in 1942," Askey said during his annual visit home in 2010. "But Austin has never left me." He never forgot his first bandleader Joyce, who came from an era when educators were bigger heroes in East Austin than footballers or singers.

Over coffee at Denny's, Askey put off questions about his glitzy musical résumé and instead told long stories of growing up dirt poor in East Austin. He made imaginary street maps with the side of his hand—"Hackberry, Juniper, Willow . . . " he'd recite.

Askey helped discover the Jackson 5 and was musical director on tours by the Four Tops, the Temptations, Gladys Knight, and the Supremes. He wrote with Curtis Mayfield and penned Linda Clifford's disco hit "Runaway Love," yet he wanted to talk more about musicians he played with on the Anderson High Yellow Jackets marching band, including Dorham, who was a year older.

Askey did not go easily from memories of Rip Ross to Diana Ross. He was writing a book about his life in his head and when asked about it, he didn't want to be rushed through the early chapters. "I'm gettin' to that," he'd say whenever a question about his career was posed, "but first I'm going to tell you the stuff people need to know about."

Askey's mother was Ada DeBlanc Simond, the noted African American historian and author who penned the "Looking Back" column in the *Austin American-Statesman* for several years. Askey's father Aubrey left when Askey was two and, with his mother already having three kids by age twenty-six, he was raised by his grandparents Gilbert and Mathilde DeBlanc, Creoles from Louisiana, who spoke French in the house.

Askey's cousin was R&B singer Damita Jo, who had minor hits with answer songs "I'll Save the Last Dance for You" (1960) and "I'll Be There," to the tune of "Stand By Me," the next year.

Joyce had recruited a ten-year-old Askey in 1935 to start playing trumpet at Kealing Middle School, whose band he also ran. "I was shooting marbles, and this kid said, 'You should try out for the band,' and I said, 'The band's for sissies. I want to play football,'" Askey recalled. Joyce overheard that exchange and within days Askey's grandmother was in Joyce's office. "He sold her an old beat-up Martin trumpet for, like, $10, and the next thing you know I'm taking lessons from Mr. Joyce."

Like most of the neighborhood kids, Askey was intimidated by Joyce, who would carry a small billy club at band practice and rap kids across the back if they were goofing off. "I came to realize he had another side to him," said Askey. "He really cared about us."

What set Askey apart from all the other horn players of East Austin was a gift for arrangement and composition that he didn't know he had until after getting out of the Army Air Corps in 1944. He enrolled first at the Boston Conservatory of Music and then the prestigious Harnett National Music Studios in Manhattan.

As an almost-required rite of passage for Texas jazz musicians, Askey played for the Houston-based Milton Larkin Orchestra for a year between those two music schools. "You could say that was the time when the trumpet took over my life," he said.

Askey started writing charts for full bands, eventually leading to his big break, a three-year stint as arranger/trumpet player with the popular Buddy Johnson band ("Since I Fell for You"). When rock 'n' roll exploded, Askey toured in the house band on package shows, backing Frankie Lymon and the Teenagers, the Platters, the Clovers, Jackie Wilson, Lloyd Price, and many more. "Bill Haley and the Comets were the only act on those tours that had their own band," Askey said.

Benjamin L.
Joyce
Service
rather than mon
is foremost
in mind

Askey received his first call from Motown on New Year's Day 1965 with an offer to produce and arrange six tracks on Billy Eckstine's *Prime of My Life*. He ended up doing the entire album.

In an attempt to broaden the Supremes' appeal in 1967, Motown mastermind Berry Gordy tapped Askey to produce *The Supremes Do Rodgers & Hart*. He also appointed him the group's musical director on live shows, including the 1970 "Farewell" performance in Las Vegas that was Ross's last show before going solo. Gordy called Askey "the glue that kept it all together."

That the Jackson 5's first album was billed *Diana Ross Presents the Jackson 5* has a connection to Askey. His stepfather Luther Simond was an assistant principal at Norton Elementary in Gary, Indiana, which some of the Jacksons had attended. Their Jackson 5 routine had instantly become a sensation in Gary and nearby Chicago, so Simond called his stepson in Detroit and said, "You need to come down here and check these guys out." Askey passed on the tip to Ross, who was having an affair with Gordy at the time.

During his Austin visits, Askey stayed with Simond, whom he called "my dad," at the house on Hamilton Avenue where his mother once cooked chitlins for the Supremes and the Manhattans on an off day on tour. "One of the girls said, 'This is good; what is this?'" Askey said, with a laugh. "I didn't have the heart to tell them that they were eating hog guts."

While touring Australia with Ross in 1973, Askey and a few other band members were caught in the rain and couldn't find a cab. A woman pulled up and gave them a ride to the hotel. Seven years later, Askey married the good Samaritan, named Hellen, and relocated to Australia, where he passed away in 2014 at age eighty-nine.

In '82, Askey flew to Los Angeles for what looked to be a month of work, helping to put together the spectacular "Motown 25" program, which featured a Supremes reunion, plus Michael Jackson's sensational moon walk to "Billie Jean." Askey's main role was arranging and conducting a soul throwdown between the Four Tops and the Temptations. Askey's month in the States turned into more than a year when a tour was thrown together after "M25."

His wife wasn't happy about that, especially having to raise an infant alone, so Askey retired from touring in 1985. He's well known in Australia through his work with programs that encourage young people to learn instruments. The former altar boy at Holy Cross Catholic Church in East Austin went to mass every Sunday.

He regretted that he was unable to get off work as music director of the movie *Fame* to attend his musical mentor's funeral in 1980. But he sent a poem, an "Ode to B. L. Joyce," which he wrote about the tailor who became one of Austin's most influential teachers.

"I could've been Gil Askey the carpenter . . . Or Gil Askey the doctor. But I became Gil Askey the musician," said the poem, which was read at the funeral. It ends with a pair of lines that have guided Askey throughout the years: "B.L. Joyce lives in the things which I do, for without him there'd be no me," it read. "Therefore, I'm an extension of him."

It was a single note, a G, that Mr. Joyce showed Askey at that first lesson, then sent him home to play only that note until he could play it perfectly. You have to start somewhere to end up anywhere.

Rupert
- Sound equals truth -

Neve

worldwide with factories in England and Scotland. In the '70s, Neve consoles became synonymous with a warm, rich, organic sound. Every studio had to have one.

Needing an infusion of capital and wanting to concentrate on design, Neve sold his company in 1975 to ESE, a corporation that made its money primarily in oil exploration. The Neves were paid mainly in company stock, and when the stock plummeted to pennies on the dollar, they virtually gave the company away. Creatively, however, Rupert Neve was on a roll. He designed the first automated console, which stored and recalled the sliding fader positions, saving producers hours of time per session.

In January 1976, Beatles producer George Martin stopped by Neve's studio to try out this new "moving fader automation," as Neve's new product was called. "We thought he might stop by for a couple hours, but he was mixing until late in the night," Neve recalls. The next day Martin sent a note: "How soon can I have one?"

An inventor without an off switch, Neve's mind is always at work, even at ninety. "Once when I was on vacation with Evelyn in Spain, I had an idea on the beach and started drawing schematics (circuit designs) on the wet sand and photographing them," he said with a laugh. "My work is my hobby." A self-taught electrical wiz, Neve started building radios as a hobby at age thirteen in Buenos Aires. He made it a business a few years later when World War II broke out and radios stopped coming from US manufacturers. Neve was able to buy the components and build radios that he sold to stores in Argentina. "Even as a boy, my product had to sound better than everybody else's," he said. "I'd listen for hours and tinker with all sorts of ways to reduce the distortion." At seventeen he joined the British Army and sailed to England.

After the war, Neve bought a US Army ambulance, which he converted into a mobile recording and public address system. His first "hit" was a policy speech by Winston Churchill, which Neve recorded straight to vinyl for worldwide release.

He met Evelyn through his sister—"sparks flew straight away"—but when he asked her father for permission to marry her, the old man said he didn't see much future in the PA system business. "You can't support my daughter in a style she's accustomed to on that kind of money," he said—so Neve moved to London and got a job designing transformers. The owner of the company also manufactured enormous loudspeaker units. "The thinking then was that quality speakers had to be huge," Neve said.

Neve designed a unit that was just as powerful but at about a quarter of the size. When the company balked on manufacturing the bookcase speakers, the Neves formed their own company, CQ Audio, in 1957. Undercapitalized, the fledgling enterprise struggled initially and there was no money to pay mounting bills. Even worse, the Neves' infant son, John, was rejecting his mother's milk and was in danger of dying of malnutrition. "I wondered what my parents would have done," Rupert said. "They would have prayed—and so about 3 a.m. one night I fell to my knees and said, 'If you're really out there, please do something.' In that instant, I could sense that someone was listening."

Although his parents were missionaries, Rupert Neve "grew up a grandson of God, not a son of God," he said. "I thought religion was for the old, the weak. I didn't need God in my life. But in that moment of clarity at 3 a.m., I realized that I'd been given a gift." The Neves' son recovered, and they've been devout Christians ever since.

"I'm not educated," Neve stated. "Nobody taught me how to do what I do. From that day forward I've never forgotten that I owe everything to God's grace. There's no other way to explain it."

Rupert and Evelyn initiated the Cambridge Radio Course in 1973 to train Christian broadcasters. It was one of his former Cambridge radio tutors whom Neve visited in Wimberley in 1980. When he returned to England, he told Evelyn that if they ever decided to move to the States, he found the perfect place, with a clean river running through it and amazingly friendly people.

The Neves invited me to seniors Bible study class at the First Baptist Church of Wimberley in 2004, when I first wrote about Rupert for the

Austin American-Statesman. It was his week to lead. "Nobody knows the Bible better than Rupert," said class leader Sue Baker. Putting on his name tag, Rupert joked that it was so he wouldn't forget his own name. But his talk was sharp, weaving Patrick Henry's defiant "give me liberty or give me death" speech of 1775 with Old Testament narratives concerning the prophet Elisha, who put himself in danger for his beliefs.

"Sometimes we have to take an aggressive action and risk the consequences," Neve said, closing his binder full of notes. "Be bold."

Wimberley is no place for the lost. When you end up here, it's meant to be.

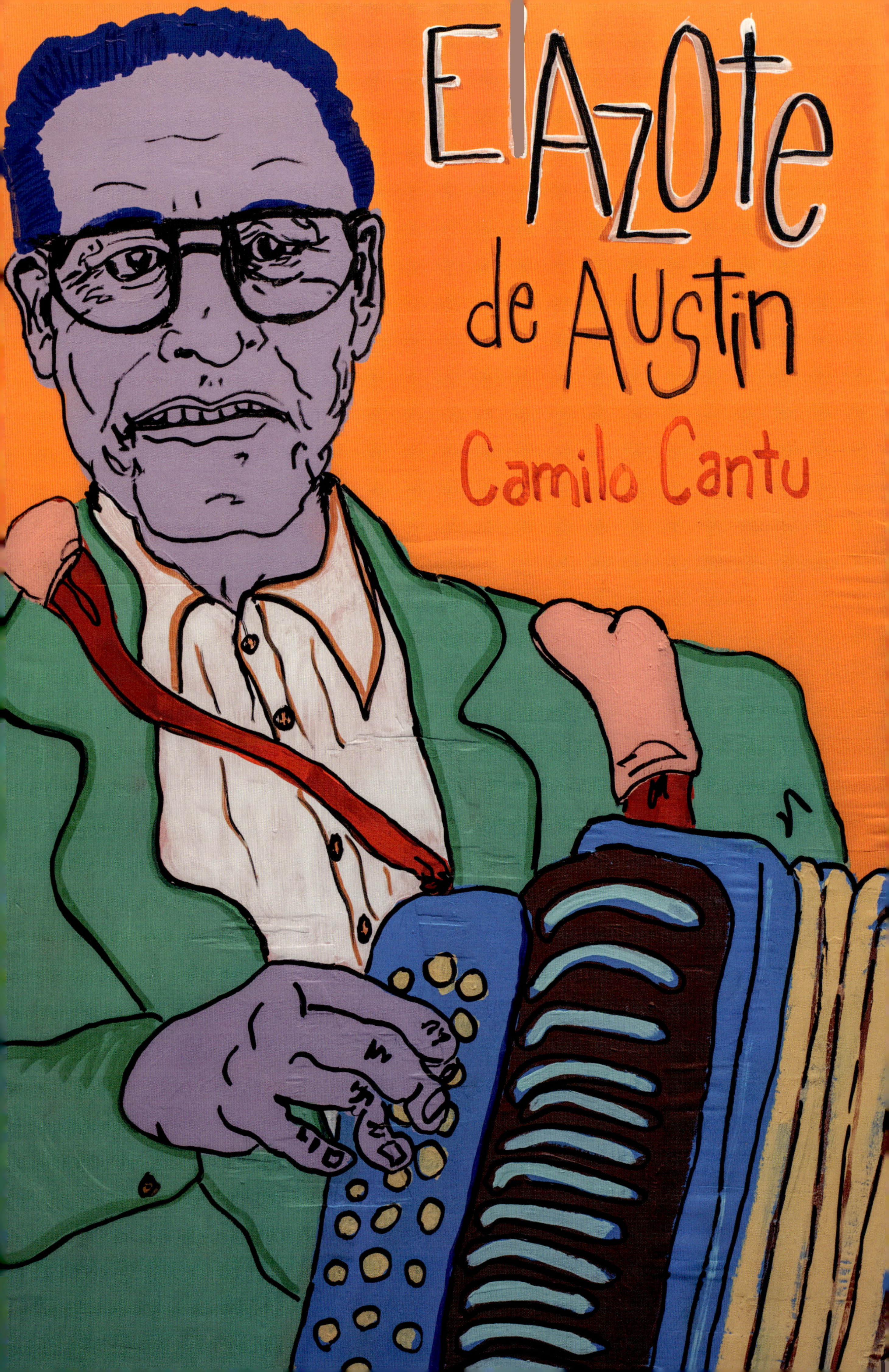
El Azote
de Austin
Camilo Cantu

CHAPTER 20

Camilo Cantu and Johnny Degollado

El Azote de Austin and El Montopolis Kid

In 1942, a seven-year-old boy accompanied his parents to La Polkita, an open-air venue in Del Valle that was basically a concrete slab outlined by Christmas lights. He became transfixed on the accordion player whose flying fingers had the power to get the whole crowd dancing. The kid couldn't believe the magic Camilo Cantu got out of that box!

Nicknamed "El Azote de Austin" ("the Scourge from Austin") because he'd go to towns and blow everybody away, Cantu was as highly regarded a player as the Big Three 1930s conjunto pioneers—Narciso Martinez, Santiago Jimenez Sr., and Valerio Longoria. But because El Azote never put out a record, retiring in 1963 to work in his accordion repair shop, he didn't become a legend. But he was a big influence on many to carry on the conjunto tradition.

"I started begging my parents for an accordion on the drive home," Degollado said about that night in '42. He got one at age ten, and by his teenaged years Degollado was leading his own group. Cantu showed him the *sordita* tuning, which gave the accordion a fuller sound, and was always happy to answer J. D.'s questions because there was nothing he loved more than lighting the torch.

In 1954, "El Montopolis Kid," as Degollado was billed, was on the road, hitting the Texas towns where the populations doubled during picking season. At a quick-stop grocery in Littlefield, near Lubbock, Degollado noticed an attractive cashier. They made clumsy small talk as he paid for his sodas, and he asked for her mailing address so he could send postcards from the road.

"Antonia," Degollado kept repeating, as he walked back to the band's station wagon. Such a pretty name. After a postcard came a love letter and a long-distance romance blossomed. During the sixth year of courtship a wedding date was set.

But Johnny's first love was the accordion, and there were disagreements about how much time he would spend out on the road. An ultimatum made him bolt, and the couple broke up in 1960.

Cantu faced a similar demand in 1963, and stayed married. No more long road trips for the Scourge, who worked every day in a repair shop attached to his house on Normandie Avenue. He was still in the music business, but now the people were coming to him, and he seemed happy. Degollado wondered if he should've done more to save the relationship with his true love.

Once, in San Antonio in the '70s, Antonia heard a song on the radio called "El Pintor" about a young couple breaking up and regretting it later, and she thought about her Johnny. When the announcer said the song was by Johnny Degollado y su Conjunto, her jaw dropped.

"I kept hoping to meet her again so I could say how sorry I was that things didn't work out," Degollado said. He got the chance in 1992, more than three decades after the split, when Toni showed up at one of his shows. "My daughter was coming through Austin on her way to San Antonio, where we lived, and she bought the Austin paper," said "Toni," as everyone calls her. "There was a picture of Johnny, and I wondered if that was my Johnny, my first boyfriend Johnny." She hadn't seen him in over thirty years. After deciding that it was, the divorced mother of four and her sister Alicia decided to go to Austin, "just to see the show, nothing else. I figured that Johnny was married and I didn't want to interfere," said Toni.

Degollado had been married, twice, and was the father of six kids, but he was single in '92. Against her sister's wishes, Alicia approached Degollado and asked if he remembered an old girlfriend named Toni. His eyes lit up.

"Well, she's sitting over there," Alicia said. The couple talked for two hours that night and married a few months later. One of their first dances as husband and wife was to a Camilo Cantu song Degollado had recorded as his own. An eighty-five-year-old Cantu looked on proudly.

"Mr. Cantu told me that if I hadn't recorded his songs, no one would ever know they existed," Degollado said in 2002, when he released *La Cajera* ("The Cashier") as a tenth anniversary gift to Toni. "He just passed them on to me and said, 'They're your songs now.'"

Taking credit for songs written by another

didn't sit well with conjunto historian and photographer Daniel Schaefer. "When J. D. recorded 'La Lupita,' one of Camilo Cantu's greatest compositions, and I saw the name 'Johnny Degollado' listed as the writer, I went to J. D. and said, 'That's not right,'" said Schaefer. "But he said that's the way the old man wanted it."

The two had an almost father-son relationship, especially after Cantu took on Degollado as an apprentice in his accordion repairing practice, which specialized in retuning new accordions by filing the reeds. "He was as talented working on accordions as he was in playing them," Degollado said.

Cantu didn't care about recognition. When he was inducted into the Conjunto Hall of Fame in 1987 at age eighty, he sent Degollado to pick up the award. The old man passed away the day before his ninety-first birthday.

At the funeral in 1998, friends fondly remembered Cantu's regular gig at Janie's Place, owned by his first wife, on East Seventh Street in Austin. Cantu didn't see the need to title his songs, which were all instrumentals. He'd start off with the melody and his bajo sexto player would fall in. But one night a drunk patron requested a certain tune by singing its melody, and Cantu couldn't take the butchering so he named it "La Calle Siete." He started naming more of his songs—or Degollado did when he recorded them later.

Degollado still has his first squeezebox, a two-row button Hohner accordion his father paid $40 for in 1945. It sits in a display case in the backyard shed where Degollado works repairing accordions and refinishing furniture. "It was important to Mr. Cantu to keep the craft alive," said Degollado. "If there's no one to fix the accordions, then people will stop playing them, and without the accordion, there's no more conjunto."

Cantu himself had a mentor in Leopoldo Guajardo, Austin's first great accordionist, who convinced Cantu to switch from keyboard accordion to a button one in 1930. Guajardo's son Santiago played guitar in Cantu's trio for years, with Felipe Rodriguez playing bass notes on the tololoche.

Known as "musica nortena" in Mexico, conjunto has thrived in the region from Monterrey, Nuevo Leon (where Cantu was born in 1907) to San Antonio since the 1930s, when Hispanic button accordion players (inspired by polkas and brass band music of Czech and German immigrants) teamed with bajo sexto guitarists to create a new sound. Narciso Martinez, from the Rio Grande Valley, practically abandoned the left-hand chord and bass buttons and instead concentrated on flashy, cat-quick runs on the treble and melody buttons controlled by his right hand. With bajo sexto player Santiago Almeida holding down the bass lines on the landmark 1936 recordings for Bluebird, the Martinez style would be adopted by almost all conjunto accordionists, except the irascible Cantu, who continued to play the buttons on both sides of the accordion and scoffed at those who didn't.

In 1947, Longoria of San Antonio added trap drums and vocals to this previously all-instrumental music, creating the precursor to contemporary Tejano music. In the '50s, Tony De La Rosa from the Corpus Christi area slowed down the Mexican polkas a little and added electric bass under his clean staccato runs. It was the heyday of conjunto, and Degollado and bajo sexto player Vicente Alonzo, who performed often on Austin's KTXN radio, would play all over Austin five or six nights a week.

But in the '60s, conjunto started getting a bad rap as poor people's music and was rivaled in popularity by a new, more sophisticated, accordion-free style called "orquesta" or "musica decente." Such still-popular acts as Little Joe y la Familia and Ruben Ramos come from the *orquesta Tejana* tradition.

"There was definitely a division. Folks who liked the orchestras hated conjunto," J. D. said. "And if you were a conjunto fan, you didn't like the orchestras." But when the newer big bands started playing and recording several Degollado compositions, including "Un Cielo" and "De Ti Estoy Enamorado," his group was able to cross over somewhat. A prolific songwriter, J. D. has penned more than one hundred songs in his career, not counting the ones Cantu taught him.

Another Great Pair of Acordeonistas

CHAPTER 21

Don Robey

Gangster of Gospel

Because the best trips end where you started, let's go back to gospel on our way home. This is the story of Houston's Don Robey—half black, half Jewish, all gangster—who did not become the first African American record mogul by playing fair. Robey put out some of the greatest gospel, R&B, and rock and roll records, starting in 1949, a decade before Berry Gordy Jr. started Motown. Duke/Peacock was raw, black Texas soul music, not aimed at crossing over to a white audience, though some of it eventually did.

As the label of the Five Blind Boys of Mississippi and the Sensational Nightingales, led by the volcanic housewreckers Archie Brownlee and Julius Cheeks, respectively, Peacock was primarily known in the early '50s as the home of hard gospel. Add the Dixie Hummingbirds from South Carolina, the Spirit of Memphis Quartet, Pilgrim Jubilee Singers from Chicago, Rev. Cleothus Robinson from Mississippi, the Brooklyn All-Stars, Sister Jessie Mae Renfro of Waxahachie, and R. H. Harris's Christland Singers, and you had one heavenly roster!

When Robey merged Peacock with Memphis R&B label Duke in 1952 (and acquired it outright the next year), his stable included Bobby "Blue" Bland, Little Junior Parker, Johnny Ace, Roscoe Gordon, Memphis Slim and some that flopped, including Joe "Mr. Google Eyes" August.

In the '60s, Peacock revolutionized gospel with the Mighty Clouds of Joy, whose choreographed moves and full band backing led to "The Temptations of Gospel" tag. Clouds lead singer Joe Ligon, who started the group in LA but moved to the Houston area after signing with Robey, was an acolyte of Brownlee and Cheeks, taking Peacock's anguished rasp sound full-circle.

Chicago was still the headquarters for black gospel music, but because of Robey's label and Buffalo Booking Agency, Houston was gospel's Second City for two decades.

It all started when Robey added a drumbeat to quartet singing with Brownlee's Blind Boys, whose fame has been surpassed by their Alabama counterparts in recent years. But back in the heyday, "The Five Blind Boys" title belonged to the guys from the Piney Wood School for the Blind near Jackson, Mississippi, who were called the Cotton Blossom Singers when Alan Lomax recorded them for the Library of Congress in 1937.

After graduation, the group began singing professionally as the Jackson Harmoneers and moved to New Orleans for better opportunities. There, they picked up fifth member

Percell Perkins and recorded obscure singles for the Excelsior and Coleman labels. They were booked in New Jersey with another blind group, and a promoter billed the concert as a battle between the Blind Boys of Mississippi and the Blind Boys of Alabama. After the show sold out, both acts ended up keeping the new names.

On tour in Houston in 1950, the Mississippi Boys met Robey, who had started Peacock a year earlier so he could put out records by management client Clarence "Gatemouth" Brown. While the first session with the "Original Five Blind Boys" did not produce a hit, the second created a monster with "Our Father." That intensifying of The Lord's Prayer, over a repetitive bass drum, was the first black gospel record to hit the jukebox. Before that, almost all quartet records were a cappella. After "Our Father" hit, almost none were.

Robey required his studio drummers to follow the beat of a red light in the studio that simulated the rhythm of a human heart. Austin gospel group the Bells of Joy had a huge hit following that formula on "Let's Talk About Jesus," which Ray Charles has cited as an influence on "I Got a Woman," the 1955 single that stole gospel's thunder—quite literally. With sales of 700,000 copies, "Let's Talk About Jesus" won the Cashbox award for best-selling religious single of 1951. The Bells had day jobs they couldn't always ditch to go tour, so Robey assembled a soundalike group to fill in on the road, when needed.

Peacock got thick in the game in 1952 when Robey signed gospel superstars the Dixie Hummingbirds, led by the inventive, charismatic Ira Tucker. The "Birds" could sing it all, exemplified by 1953 smash "Let's Go Out to the Programs," in which the group delivered perfect imitations of the Soul Stirrers, the Five Blind Boys, the Pilgrim Travelers, the Bells of Joy, and, lastly, the Dixie Hummingbirds.

Peacock's other big signing in '52 was the Sensational Nightingales, assembled in North Carolina by former Hummingbird Barney

Parks a few years earlier. Besides Cheeks, whom Wilson Pickett acknowledged as a primary influence, the 'gales added two other lead singers—Ernest James and Jo Jo Wallace—before making their Peacock debut in the summer of '52. The Nightingales' most sensational number was 1956's "Burying Ground," with Cheeks's seismic vocals burying all contenders.

Before 1956, when a full studio was built at 2809 Erastus, Robey and musical directors Joe Scott and Dave Clark used Bill Holford's ACA (Audio Company of America) studio on Westheimer. Peacock artists were in and out of there all the time, as Robey kept signing acts like the Southern Wonders, Christian Travelers, Stars of Hope, Golden Harps, and Gospelaires.

If anyone had a problem with Robey's sketchy concept of remuneration, they weren't on Peacock for long. Ira Tucker told interviewer Seamus McGarvey years later that he never really had a problem with the entrepreneur whose very name started with R-O-B. "The only thing that you had to watch was, if you had a deal with Don, you had to keep him with the deal (because) if he could talk you out of it, he would," he said. "If he could scare you down, he would."

Roscoe Robinson, who in 1960 replaced Archie Brownlee as lead singer of the Five Blind Boys of Mississippi after the great shouter died of pneumonia at age thirty-five, said Robey paid the group with a new car and performing uniforms, but they never received royalties. Like all Peacock acts, they made their money on the road.

"When our contract was up, we asked Robey for a new car and he said 'no,' so we signed with Chess Records up in Chicago," said Robinson, who was eighty-eight in 2017. But after the Five Blind Boys made a record for Chess subsidiary Checker Records in '62, Robey had a scheme to defraud Chess by producing a contract with the Blind Boys that he had back-dated.

"He said he would cut us in on a lot of money (Peacock sued Chess for $450,000) if we signed the contract, but me and Shorty (Abrams) refused, so they kicked us out of the group," said Robinson.

Getting paid to do something you love was a novel concept after the Depression and WWII, and that sentiment fueled impresario greed across the board in the music business at the time. What was important was that Robey allowed musicians to make records, and the style didn't matter as long as people were buying them.

Robey had four labels in all, including Back Beat, which took Roy Head's "Treat Her Right" to #2 on the *Billboard* pop singles chart in 1965, outselling everyone but the Beatles.

Before it served as headquarters for Peacock Records, the 2809 Erastus Street address in the Fifth Ward housed Robey's sophisticated Bronze Peacock Dinner Club from 1945 to '51. There also was a very active back room for gambling. But after "Our Father" hit, Robey and his savvy business (and sometime romantic) partner Evelyn Johnson started phasing out the costly club and concentrating on the music business.

Peacock had its first hit R&B smash with Big Mama Thornton's "Hound Dog" in 1953, predating the sensational Elvis Presley cover by three years. Blues acts were tapping into the intensity of gospel to create the rock 'n' roll sensation, and Robey was right there, hitting again with "Pack Fair and Square" by Big Walter and His Thunderbirds. Inspired by the Duke/Peacock success, a black couple from Gary, Indiana, named Vivian and James Bracken founded Vee-Jay in 1953 to put out "Baby It's You" by the Spaniels and Jimmy Reed records. The label became prominent in the early '60s with #1 records by the Beatles and the Four Seasons, but the white acts had lawyers and sued an overwhelmed Vee-Jay, which didn't have the resources to keep up with the demand, over back royalties. The label folded in 1966, though it was revived under new management for a few years in the '80s.

Peacock was not the country's first black-owned label: Harry Pace's Black Swan (1921-1923) had moderate success with Ethel Waters and Alberta Hunter but no hits. Robey kept Duke/Peacock alive and thriving for almost twenty-five years. Among the #1 R&B hits: "I Pity the Fool" and "Further on Up the Road" by Bobby Bland, "Next Time You See Me" by Junior Parker, and "Pledging My Love" by Johnny Ace, a posthumous smash after Ace

Season's Greetings

DUKE-PEACOCK FAMILY

INCORPORATED

2809 ERASTUS STREET
PHONES: OR 3-1225 - OR 3-2611
DON D. ROBEY HOUSTON, TEXAS 77026

accidentally killed himself playing with a gun backstage on Christmas Day, 1954.

By the early '60s, Peacock had so many gospel artists on the roster that Robey started a new religious music subsidiary Song Bird. Some of Robey's earlier competitors, such as the Specialty, Apollo, and Gotham labels, had become inactive, so he was signing just about anyone he wanted and at one point had 109 acts under contract, according to Ray Funk's 1990 history of Peacock's gospel division that ran in *Rejoice!* magazine (an invaluable source for this chapter).

The gospel side paid unexpected dividends when Tennessee native O. V. Wright, a former member of the Sunset Travelers, had a huge secular hit in 1964 with "That's How Strong My Love Is" on the Goldwax label. Robey discovered that Wright was still under contract to him, so he claimed the rising R&B star for his Back Beat label and had big hits with "Eight Men, Four Women" and "A Nickel and a Nail." If there was money to be made, Robey was on it.

By the late '60s, he was spending more and more time at his ranch near Crosby, where he raised thoroughbreds and practiced for rodeos. As a metaphor to his time in music, Robey's specialty was calf-roping.

When he hit seventy years old in 1973, Don Robey sold his assets, which included 2,700 song copyrights (several hundred co-"written" by Deadric Malone, his pen name), to ABC/Dunhill for an undisclosed amount. His last hit was a gospel number, "Lord Don't Move That Mountain," by Inez Andrews on Song Bird.

Don Robey did have a heart, it turned out, and it stopped beating in 1975. He made a lot of money off the talents of others because that was the game. But he was also responsible for some of the most soulful sounds of the '50s and '60s, split evenly between the spiritual and the secular.

"He might've ripped me off," Gatemouth Brown said in 2005, "but if it wasn't for Don Robey, nobody would've ever heard of me."

BONUS TRACK:

A Dozen More Worth a Deep Dive

Charline Arthur (Henrietta) recorded rockabilly and boogie-woogie in the late '40s with Dallas producer Jim Beck, then signed to RCA. She was managed by Colonel Tom Parker, whose entire attention would soon go to a new client.

Larry Graham (Beaumont) invented slap-popping funk bass with his cousin Sly (Stewart) and the Family Stone. Graham played with Prince for years before the fellow Jehovah's Witness's April 2016 death.

Peck's Bad Boys (Houston) featured the great teenaged trombonist Jack Teagarden, who called bandleader Peck Kelley "the greatest piano player in the world." The shy Kelley refused to leave his humble Houston home for the jazz havens of New Orleans, Chicago, or New York in the 1920s and instead drew top players to him, including Louis Prima and Pee Wee Russell.

Rudy "Tee" Gonzales (San Antonio) was an architect of the "Westside Sound" (Royal Jesters, Sunny and the Sunliners) in the '50s as leader of the Reno Bops. As of 2018 he was still performing his high energy Mexican R&B.

Victoria Spivey (Houston) wrote and recorded "Black Snake Blues" in 1926, before Blind Lemon Jefferson stole it, then starred in King Vidor's 1929 all-black film *Hallelujah*. The blues diva came out of retirement during the '60s folk music revival and hired a kid named Bob Zimmerman to play harmonica on her last record.

Ray Sharpe (Fort Worth) is a black rockabilly singer/guitarist who wrote and recorded 1959's "Linda Lu" (produced by Lee Hazlewood), a minor hit covered by major acts like the Rolling Stones and the Flying Burrito Brothers. We've heard many a story about the white act everyone thought was black. Sharpe flipped that.

The Offenders (Austin) with J. J. on vocals, Tony on guitar, Mikey on bass, and Pat on drums were the most ferocious punk band in 1980's Texas, an equal in intensity to any touring hardcore band they opened for, or who opened for them. Their "I Hate Myself" is a standout on the 1983 Texas punk collection *Cottage Cheese from the Lips of Death*.

Jimmy Heap and the Melody Masters (Taylor) recorded the original versions of "Wild Side of Life" and "Release Me." Pianist Arlie Carter cowrote "Wild Side," which Hank Thompson had a huge hit with in 1952.

Don Brooks (Dallas) set the standard for outlaw country harmonica with Waylon Jennings in '73 and '74, mentoring Willie's longtime harpman Mickey Raphael. The master of tone and rhythm passed away at fifty-three from leukemia.

Hop Wilson (Grapeland), backed only by drummer Ivory Lee Semien, made some wild steel guitar blues records for Goldband, inspiring a host of slide players as well as raw neo-Delta acts like the White Stripes and Jon Spencer Blues Explosion.

Willie Neal Johnson (Tyler) was nicknamed "The Country Boy" because he grew up on a farm six miles outside of Tyler, but his singing with the Gospel Keynotes was pure Pentecostal soul. Though Johnson never reached the popularity of rivals, the Mighty Clouds of Joy, Joe Ligon's group couldn't top the Keynotes version of "Jesus Is on the Mainline" from 1994. YouTube it! The singer/bandleader died of a stroke in 2001 at age sixty-five.

Marijohn Wilkin (Kemp) had her first two songwriting credits released on the same day in 1959: "Long Black Veil" by Lefty Frizzell and Stonewall Jackson's "Waterloo." She also gave Kris Kristofferson his first writing gig with her publishing house and cowrote "Cut Across Shorty" for Eddie Cochran and "I Just Don't Understand" by Ann-Margret, which the Beatles covered.

About the Author

Michael Corcoran, shown here with Joe Ely and Butch Hancock of the Flatlanders, has been covering Texas music since 1984, first as an acerbic columnist for the *Austin Chronicle*, then as a music critic for the *Dallas Morning News*. More recently, he's been a musical detective whose book/CDs about gospel curiosities Arizona Dranes and Washington Phillips received "best historical album" Grammy nominations in 2012 and 2016, respectively. A native of Honolulu, Corcoran found his true paradise in the richly diverse and wholly original landscape of Texas music.

Ornette Coleman
I find that labels are the worst thing in the world for artistic expression

Artist Tim Kerr

This book's illustrator could very well have been a subject as a Texas music pioneer. His first band, the Big Boys, mixed funk and punk to presage the Red Hot Chili Peppers, but his next group, Poison 13, although not as popular, was even more influential. Seattle college DJ Mark Arm of Green River (and later Mudhoney) played their bluesy Sabbath thrash, and listeners Kurt Cobain, Mike McCready, Kim Thayil, and others heard a new way to be loud. There were more bands—Bad Mutha Goose, Monkeywrench, Lord High Fixers, Now Time Delegation, not to mention more than two dozen production credits. But these days the category-defying musician mainly banjos the valleys of mountain music with friends.

Kerr's self-expressionism has always included a visual arts side since he won an elementary school drawing contest in his native Lake Jackson, where the Kerr men are known as high school football coaches, not skateboarding punk rockers. Kerr the guitarist made use of his painting degree from the University of Texas when he was commissioned in 2012 to paint an 8-foot-tall mural of Negro League baseball star Willie Wells, an Austin native. In 2015, Kerr had a solo exhibit at the Rosa Parks Museum in Birmingham, Alabama—a career highpoint. His artwork has been shown in NYC, London, Berlin, Chicago, Tokyo and Texas, of course.

"I live my life with my five senses wide open," he recently told an interviewer about how he moves so easily between music and art. "I'm hoping I haven't seen or heard the best thing yet."

Index